She Leads

GOD'S INTENT FOR
WOMEN IN THE CHURCH

Robbie Cansler

f·

THE FOUNDRY
PUBLISHING·

Cover designer: Caines Design
Interior designer: Sharon Page

Library of Congress Cataloging-in-Publication Data
A complete catalog record for this book is available from the Library of
Congress.

The internet addresses, email addresses, and phone numbers in this
book are accurate at the time of publication. They are provided as a
resource. The Foundry Publishing does not endorse them or vouch for
their content or permanence.

CONTENTS

$\longleftrightarrow$

INTRODUCTION

←→

Our views on women in leadership roles come from a variety of places. Some of us grew up watching women lead in various places and spaces—in our homes, in our schools, and in the church. Some of us have heard repeatedly that women should be silent in church, or that they can't lead, and we have been formed by these words even if we aren't entirely sure where they come from. Some of us are unsure of where women should occupy leadership positions, and we wonder if Scripture has anything to say about it.

Regardless of our starting point, we all have opinions and thoughts on women in leadership. The Wesleyan-Holiness tradition supports the leadership of women in all areas of the church from preaching to teaching, from the home to the church office to ordained ministry, and all the way to the highest offices of the church. Where did this practice come from? Are the Wesleyan-Holiness beliefs about women in ministry cultural, or is there more to it than that?

These questions are exactly what this book seeks to answer. Together we will walk through Scripture, theology, and church history to explore why women can and should be leading in all areas of the church and to discover and affirm that we can feel comfortable supporting and advocating for women who are called by God to serve the church in various leadership positions.

Reading the Bible and understanding it can be a daunting task. If you were asked to pick up a different ancient text that is thousands of years old, read it, understand it, and then apply it to your life, you might at least hesitate if not reject the request completely! Most of us don't spend our lives studying various ancient texts. It is probably fair to say that most of us don't even understand the languages of ancient texts. Yet studying and understanding is the task we are given when we pick up the Bible.

There are barriers to reading Scripture and understanding it fully—barriers of time, culture, language, and more. These barriers are often compounded by the reality that we all bring our own biases, experiences, personal challenges, and hang-ups to the text. Yet we still believe the Bible is a unique text that has been inspired by God and given to us to point us *to* God so that we might live a life of faithfulness. Therefore, crossing those barriers and wrestling with the challenges is important and necessary work.

Because we live with the realities of barriers and challenges, when we pick up a book about a topic like women in leadership, it can be hard to know where to begin. Where do we focus? What do we do with texts that feel out of place? How do we discern between what our own biases are and what God is saying? There are some helpful things to keep in mind as we do the work of biblical interpretation together.

We first want to approach Scripture with prayer, expressing openness for the Holy Spirit to say something to us, even if it is uncomfortable. We believe that Scripture is unique in that the Holy Spirit was at work when it was written, at work when it was collected into the sixty-six books we know as the canon of Scripture, and at work within us when we read it, interpret it, and apply it to our lives. This is the first and most important step in doing this work. We approach Scripture with humility, and with the expectation that the Holy Spirit has something to say to us.

We then want to make sure we are looking at the cultural, historical, and textual contexts for the passages we are walking through. Context helps us get a better understanding of what the authors intended for readers and listeners to hear. There is a barrier for us of thousands of years, not to mention usually geographical and cultural gaps, and it is important for us to acknowledge these gaps and barriers and work through them well. Context can also help ensure that we aren't making the text say something different than it means to say.

When we read Scripture, we always want to look at the parts in light of the whole. Scripture in its entirety is telling us a story about God, and about who we are called to be in light of who God is. While that story is told in particular parts, looking at only the parts without looking at the big picture will give us an inaccurate image of who God is and who we are called to be in light of that.

The last helpful component of good biblical interpretation is to do the work in community. Reading Scripture together and dialoguing with other Christians helps us do the work more faithfully. For that very reason, this book is intended to be read and discussed in a group. We are better when we do this work collectively. The church is not meant to be a group of loosely assembled individuals but a community that comes together as the body of Christ.

Good biblical interpretation doesn't exist in a vacuum. It is important that we also work in conjunction with a foundation of good theology. The Wesleyan Quadrilateral is the helpful theological tool we use when working through a Wesleyan-Holiness lens. It is not perfect, but it can help us as we wrestle with the topic of women in leadership. The Wesleyan Quadrilateral says there are four things that help us know God more faithfully and fully: Scripture, reason, tradition, and experience. We give the most primary space to Scripture *while* understanding that we can't understand Scripture well without the other three. The four components together help us navigate the barriers and challenges before us, and they also help us to know God more fully.

Theology is, most simply, "the study of God." As we wrestle with biblical texts, we must also wrestle with our theology. What we believe about God informs what we believe about ourselves, about others, and about the ways that God interacts with us and the world. Wesleyans believe in some important theological truths, like prevenient grace—the grace that goes before—which means we believe the Holy Spirit is at work in the world before we show up and that all people are called to follow God. We also believe that God's primary motivation is love. Rooted in scriptures like John 3:16 ("For God so loved the world") and 1 John 4:8 and 4:16 ("God is love"), we view one of the primary characteristics of God as love. We also believe in the work of sanctification—that God seeks to make us more and more like God and that ultimately, through the power of the Holy Spirit, we are freed from the bondage of sin in our lives and transformed into Christlikeness.

With these frameworks in mind, I have a few questions I'd like you to ask yourself before you even begin reading the rest of this book. These questions are meant to help you work through some of these barriers and challenges in your own heart and mind. Before you look at the questions, take time to pray that the Holy Spirit would be present with you, would help you be honest with yourself, and would help you be open to the work God wants to do in you.

Once you have taken time to read through the questions, think about them, and answer them, take some time to share your answers with your group. Remember that we are on this journey together, and we are all starting from different places. We want space to wrestle deeply, so cultivate space in your group for the possibility of disagreement or even mild conflict. Don't avoid it! Instead, embrace it in a healthy way, understanding that it can help us become more faithful followers of Jesus together.

QUESTIONS FOR REFLECTION AND DISCUSSION

1. Where do your ideas about women in leadership come from? What has formed your ideas about women in leadership the most?

2. Have you heard sermons or read books about women in leadership before? What has your response to those sermons or books been?

3. Have you interacted with women in Christian leadership, and how did you feel in and after those interactions?

4. When have you learned from a woman in a leadership position?

5. What do you personally believe about women in leadership as you start this book?

6. How open are you to what the Holy Spirit may want to show you about women in leadership?

1
LEADERSHIP
IN THE HOME
←→

There may be no better place to start looking at women in leadership in the Bible than in the beginning. Genesis 1:26–27 (CEB) says, "Then God said, 'Let us make humanity in our image to resemble us so that they may take charge of the fish of the sea, the birds in the sky, the livestock, all the earth, and all the crawling things on earth.' God created humanity in God's own image, in the divine image God created them, male and female God created them." The creation narrative sets an important foundation for the belief that women should be included in all levels of leadership within the church because we see that both men and women were created in the image of God at the very creation of humanity.

Both women and men are image bearers in the world, reflecting who God is to the world around them. Nijay Gupta says it this way in his book *Tell Her Story*:

Both are fashioned in the image of God (Gen. 1:26–27); not Adam, then Eve, but both together reflect God. Both are blessed and are given the responsibility of ruling the earth (Gen. 1:26, 28). Both are given the fruit of the earth for food and enjoyment (Gen. 1:29–30). While they are distinguished according to two types, male and female, nothing in Genesis 1 distinguishes the two in their God-given identity, calling, and relationship to other parts of creation. If all we knew of creation came from this chapter, we would conceive of man and woman as equals, partners and co-rulers on earth as the image of God.

Equality is the starting line and the foundation of creation. This perfect garden that sin had yet to touch was one where women and men were equals.

HELPER/HELPMEET/EZER KENEGDO

Despite this foundation—that both men and women are created in God's image—there is a pervasive belief that, since man was created first, according to the Genesis 2 narrative, man is superior to woman, and women were created to be a helper to men rather than equals. This idea is perpetuated by the hierarchical idea that men are to be over women for all of time and that, although women are also created in the image of God, they are distinctly different from, and therefore belong below, men.

When we examine the biblical text more closely, however, we find that it does not support this interpretation. Genesis 2:18 says, "The LORD God said, 'It is not good for the man to be alone. I will make a helper suitable for him.'" The word translated as "helper" in this verse is *ezer kenegdo* in Hebrew. There are various translations of this word, with "helper" being the most prominent, but Lucy Peppiatt shares in her book the thoughts of R. David Freedman on this Hebrew phrase:

The customary translation ["helper"] of these two words [*ezer kenegdo*], despite its near universal adoption, is wrong. That is not what the words are intended to convey. They should be translated instead to mean approximately "a power equal to man." That is, when God concluded that he would create another creature so that man would not be alone, he decided to make "a power equal to him," someone whose strength was equal to man's. Woman was not intended to be merely man's helper. She was meant instead to be his partner.

The word *ezer* is used in Scripture sixteen different times to describe God. God is obviously not subordinate to humanity, yet the term that is often translated as "helper" in reference to women is the same word that is used for God elsewhere. Therefore, it cannot mean subordinate and does not indicate a lower hierarchical position; rather, "strong help" might be a more appropriate way to think of it. Understanding the meaning of the Hebrew phrasing helps us understand that women were never meant to be subservient to men but equal to them. Men and women were both created in God's image, as equals before God, to reflect the image of God in the world.

It is important to note that this equality before God and the world is the precursor to the fall. The creation narratives take place in Genesis 1 and 2, and the fall happens in chapter 3. The intended state of relationships for men and women was one of partnership and equality, but things become distorted and disordered when sin enters the picture. The idea of a man-over-woman hierarchy is itself a consequence of the fall. We see this laid out in Genesis 3:16, where God says to Eve, "I will make your pains in childbearing very severe; with painful labor you will give birth to children. Your desire will be for your husband, and he will rule over you." In the New Beacon Bible Commentary on Genesis, Joseph Coleson emphasizes that this consequence is not of God's choosing, nor was it God's original intention for the relationship between humans: "Genesis 3:16 is God's announcement of this tragic fracturing: the man's grabbing for himself the power of the stewardship dominion mandate, and his exercise of it upon and against the woman." At times, Christians have interpreted Genesis 3:16 as how things are meant to be, with the husband ruling over his wife, and all men ruling over all women, but it is instead a consequence of the fall.

Hierarchy is simply one of many ways that sin destroys relationships. In fact, this fracturing of relationships due to sin is illustrated in the ways Adam and Eve blame each other as well. Some have used the proof of Eve eating the fruit first as another reason that women should live subserviently to men. The argument is sometimes made that women were created weaker, or less wise, but the picture painted in Genesis 3 of casting blame happens only after sin has entered the picture.

When God walks in the garden to find them, the response is not one of confession, repentance, and restoration. Instead, they rush to blame each other and God. What might have been different for these first humans if, instead of hiding in shame and rushing to blame, they confessed their sin? We are told in 1 John 1:9 of a God who is faithful and just to forgive us our sins, which leads me to believe that forgiveness available to Adam and Eve as well. As we confess and repent, we find forgiveness and a life of freedom. Our lives are not supposed to be lived under the rule of sin; instead, they are to be reordered to reflect God's intention for us, which is equality. We are to live, in the words of John 12:36, as children of the light.

This view of sin is particularly important for Holiness people, who believe strongly that we live under the grace of Jesus and are therefore no longer slaves to sin. Paul lays out this theology for us clearly in Romans 6:1–4: "What shall we say, then? Shall we go on sinning so that grace may increase? By no means! We are those who have died to sin; how can we live in it any longer? Or don't you know that all of us who were baptized into Christ Jesus were baptized into his death? We were therefore buried with him through baptism into death in order that, just as Christ was raised from the dead through the glory of the Father, we too may live a new life." We are not to live as people of sin any longer but as people who are free. We are to live life the way God intended, which includes the equality of men and women. Dr. Coleson says,

> One of the strongest themes of a Wesleyan approach to Scripture is that the fruits of our redemption in Christ begin already to be realized here on this earth. If that can be true anywhere, surely it can be true in the home of the man and woman committed to living as believers in Christ, and within the gatherings of the body of believers called the church. With other Christians, Wesleyans should live intentionally, and in every way possible, the "already" of creation's restoration in Christ, even as we anticipate the "not yet" of his return.

When women are placed in a hierarchy as less than or below men, we return to living under the consequences of sin and death. Scripture instead challenges us to "live lives worthy of God, who calls you into his kingdom and glory" (1 Thessalonians 2:12b). As children of light and people of the kingdom of God, we are called to live as equals regardless of gender.

QUESTIONS FOR DISCUSSION OR REFLECTION

1. What are your thoughts on the meaning of *ezer kenegdo* shared in this section?

2. How does your understanding of the term "helper" or "help-meet" change when you see that the Hebrew term those words come from is defined as "a power equal to man"?

3. What do you think about the picture the author has painted of man and woman before the fall, and of how sin changed that picture?

HEAD/KEPHALĒ

The misinterpretation of the hierarchy of man over woman in Genesis 2 is often exacerbated by its connection to 1 Corinthians 11:2–10. This section of scripture is one of the places where the idea of "headship" comes from—that the man is to be head over his wife and family. The idea is connected with Genesis because of verse 3 in particular: "But I want you to realize that the head of every man is Christ, and the head of the woman is man, and the head of Christ is God." The original Greek word for the word "head" in 1 Corinthians 11 is *kephalē*. *Kephalē* is often defined as "head," but it can also mean "ruler, leader, person in authority, foremost, one who is preeminent, and source." Because of these numerous definitions, we can't be completely sure which one Paul intended in this text.

It has often been assumed that Paul meant a hierarchy—that men are to be over women as leaders in both the home and the church. There is a glaring issue with this interpretation, though, since the phrase "the head of Christ is God" appears in the same sentence. As Trinitarian people, we believe that God the Father, God the Son, and God the Spirit are three-in-one. They are three distinct yet equal beings who are also one. Wesleyans believe there is no hierarchy in the Trinity. This idea of man as the head of woman is partnered with God being the head of Christ.

If there is no hierarchy in the Trinity, then it makes sense to conclude that Paul's intent for men and women here isn't hierarchy but something else. In light of this understanding, it makes more sense to interpret *kephalē* here as "source" instead of "head." Genesis tells us that woman was made *from* man. Although we don't believe that Jesus was made *from* God, we do talk about Christ as the "begotten" Son of God, and of Jesus as being *sent from* God. Therefore, "source" is a more likely interpretation, which rests in harmony with Genesis and respects God's creational intent of equality between men and women. We see this idea emphasized later in the same 1 Corinthians passage in verse 12: "For as woman came from man, so also man is born of woman. But everything comes from God." This verse points to our ultimate source, whether we are man or woman, as being God, while also showing a unique interdependence that men and women have with each other.

Another important context for these verses (remember that we look at the particular in light of the whole) is 1 Corinthians 12, which focuses on the church as the body of Christ. The body does not have a hierarchy of the head over the rest of the body. In fact, Lucy Peppiatt points out:

> Paul's teaching here is not simply that they should be honoring those who are perceived to be inferior, but that there is a God-ordained reversal of status in the body of Christ. But *God has adjusted the body*, giving greater honor to

the inferior part. What is the purpose of God having done this? That there may be no discord in the body, but that the members may have the same care for one another. If one member suffers, all suffer together; if one member is honored/glorified, all rejoice together. . . . He warns those who perceive themselves to be in position of the head that they may never say to any other part of the body, "I have no need of you." . . . Far more radically, Paul claims that those who are more "important" must devote themselves to honoring the dishonorable parts in the knowledge that those members are the ones accorded the highest honor by God himself.

First Corinthians 12 does not lay out an image of a hierarchy where one person, or even an entire group of people, is given charge to reign over another. It is an egalitarian picture of mutual respect and care, where each person is celebrated for their gifts and talents, and everyone is tasked with caring for the others.

QUESTIONS FOR DISCUSSION OR REFLECTION

1. How have you seen the word "head" defined in the past in gender relationships?

2. How does this explanation of the Greek word *kephalē* change your understanding of the translation and meaning of "head" in relation to a marriage?

3. What are your thoughts on "source" as a translation for *kephalē* instead of "head"?

SUBMISSION

There is also an image of this mutual care, specifically in marriage, in 1 Corinthians 7: "The wife does not have authority over her own body but yields it to her husband. In the same way, the husband does not have authority over his own body but yields it to his wife. Do not deprive each other except perhaps by mutual consent and for a time, so that you may devote yourselves to prayer. Then come together again so that Satan will not tempt you because of your lack of self-control" (vv. 4–5). Again, this is not an image of hierarchy but of mutuality. The wife and husband are both instructed to yield, and the decision to deprive each other is done by mutual consent, not by command and submission. This passage of mutuality in marriage stands out starkly against the patriarchal culture of the time—a culture in which women didn't have the right to consent to sexual relations. The very idea of a woman's agency to consent would have been foreign. Paul's instruction that women had the same authority over their husbands' bodies that men had over theirs, and the idea of mutuality in both sexual congress and deprivation, would have been radical for the time period and cultural setting.

This 1 Corinthians 7 passage is still important for us today, especially given the knowledge that throughout history women have not been allowed to refuse their husbands' sexual advances, and marital rape wasn't legally acknowledged. In fact, in the United States marital rape didn't become illegal in all fifty states until July 5, 1993. We know there are still places in our world where the rights of women to their own bodies are nonexistent. This broken reality is a consequence of sin. Paul's directives to husbands and wives toward mutual care and consent feel radical for the ancient patriarchal world, but they are still radical in much of our own world today, where the sin of sexual violence still heavily ravages and victimizes especially women and girls. These realities make it all the more important for the people of God to get this issue right. When we live as though the kingdom of God is realized now, we are free to create systems and advocate for justice in ways that are life-giving for women and girls around the world.

This idea of mutual consent extends beyond sexual relations. Some complementarians in the church have posed the question to egalitarians: if there is no hierarchy in a marriage, who casts the deciding vote when a couple cannot agree? When we examine this question through the lens of 1 Corinthians 7, we see that Paul seems to emphasize the possibility of mutual decision making. It isn't about a hierarchy where one person is in charge; instead, it is a co-leading and reciprocity that looks like mutual care and conversation. This type of marriage is not meant to be the exception but the norm within the church.

Men are not meant to be the sole leader in the home, with wives in a hierarchy under them. Instead, men and women, husbands and wives, are meant to work together as they both submit to Christ. Women and men are called to live into their gifts in the body of Christ, which includes in the home as well, taking leadership in the areas in which they are each gifted to lead and working together as partners.

Another difficult text when talking about hierarchy in the home is Ephesians 5:22–24: "Wives, submit yourselves to your own husbands as you do to the Lord. For the husband is the head of the wife as Christ is the head of the church, his body, of which he is the Savior. Now as the church submits to Christ, so also wives should submit to their husbands in everything." This passage might be the first one that comes to people's minds when marriage in the church comes up. Many traditions used to have a line in marriage vows when the bride would have to commit to submission or obedience to her new husband. These commitments to submission and obedience are rightfully excluded from traditional vows in the Wesleyan tradition; instead, the focus is on mutual care for each other.

Ephesians 5 has been preached regularly in defense of hierarchy in the home and, at times, has been used to defend abuse. The term "submission" on its own has become synonymous with quiet wives who do not have the right to their own opinion or thoughts and who don't cause trouble for anyone. Sometimes the word "submission" alone reminds women of a traumatic past where the word was weaponized against them, whether within a marriage or in the church. It has become a word that has often been wielded like a sword to keep women from assuming positions of leadership in the home or beyond.

With all of the baggage that comes along with Ephesians 5 and the word "submission," we ought to take time to dive deeply into what this word, and the text we find it in, actually means. Does it mean women are to be subservient to men? Or is something different going on here? Cultural context can help us answer this question. There is a divide of more than two thousand years between the culture of the New Testament and our culture today, which means there are some dramatic differences. New Testament scholar Lynn Cohick reminds us in her commentary on Ephesians:

> The wide gulf separating our society from the ancient one requires readers to be careful exegetes, discerning what the biblical text describes or takes for granted within their social world and what the apostle prescribes as fitting for all human cultures within their local churches. Isolating the ancient culture, then ascertaining Paul's affirmation of our challenge to it, will help us discover applications for these texts in our contexts.

One of those differences is that, in the ancient Greco-Roman world (the world in which Ephesians and the other epistles take place), families were organized around the concept of *paterfamilias*. *Paterfamilias* is a Latin term that means "the father of families." The family was organized in a patriarchal way around the father of a household. Heirs were decided through the father's lineage, and the father maintained wealth and passed it on to his sons—not to his wife, not to his daughter(s). In this way, the Roman empire could ensure that wealthy Roman families married other wealthy Roman families and produced good Roman children, which was beneficial to the expansion and well-being of the empire.

In the Greco-Roman world of *paterfamilias*, there were household codes and laws that helped guide how families were ordered. Ephesians 5 is a household code written in a similar pattern to those produced by the empire, but it looks different. One of the most noticeable differences, according to the New Beacon Bible Commentary on Ephesians, is that "Roman law made no restrictions on [the husband/father/master's] governance. But Paul severely regulated his exercise of power." It is taken for granted in the Ephesians text that the man has the power and status, which is an important starting point for us because, while Roman household codes maintained the power of men, Paul's Christian household code does something different.

Before diving into what the Ephesians household code says or doesn't say, let's look first at the structure of the verses. Often in our modern English versions of this passage, there is a division between verse 20 and verse 21 that doesn't exist in the original Greek. In fact, Ephesians 5:21—"Submit to one another out of reverence for Christ"—is an incomplete sentence that concludes the preceding section and is connected to the command that begins in in verse 18: "Be filled with the Spirit." This distinction indicates that submitting to one another is done as a response to being filled with the Spirit, and it is a posture that is expected of all Christians as they learn to live in community together.

Then we have verses 22–24, which George Lyons's NBBC commentary on Ephesians helps illuminate for us. Even though the verb "submit" is used in both verse 22 and verse 24 in our English translations, there is in fact no verb used in those verses in the Greek text, except in the case of "submits" appearing in verse 24 in reference to the relationship between Christ and the church. Paul never explicitly commands wives to obey their husbands. Paul never uses any imperatives toward wives, yet husbands are commanded twice to love their wives (vv. 25 and 33), and are told once that they "ought to love" their wives (v. 28). Lynn Cohick explains that the use of these imperatives directed toward the husband likely reflects the cultural reality that the husband is the one who has the power and ability to change the marriage relationship. Lyons adds,

> Within a patriarchal society, a submissive husband was unthinkable. Within each of the three pairs [husband/ wife, father/children, master/slave], the *paterfamilias* was the dominant figure—the husband, father, and master. Greco-Roman culture could not conceive of a master who would humble himself, be obedient, allow himself to be shamed, or be submissive to his subjects. But the gospel of Jesus Christ offered an alternate vision of reality. Paul announced the good news of a God whose power, glory, and wisdom were demonstrated in the weakness, shame, and folly of the cross. . . . Christ, not culture, shapes Christian households.

Even though it was unthinkable to call a husband to submit in the cultural setting of the time, Paul has commanded husbands to love their wives with such strong wording that, in verse 25, he says "as Christ loved the church," emphasizing that husbands are to love in a self-sacrificial way, being willing to lay down their lives for their wives, which would indeed be a countercultural commandment.

We also see this countercultural disposition in the use of the word "head" in verse 23. The word here is once again *kephalē*, which we have now learned *could* mean something akin to a hierarchical leader, yet scholars have concluded that in this context it most likely means something along the lines of "source." Interestingly, says Cohick, in the culture of the time, "the expectation would be that the body sacrifices itself for the head—a conclusion directly at odds with the gospel message . . . Christ the head of the church in love laid down his life for his beloved (5:2)." The prevailing cultural assumption would be that wives should sacrifice for their husbands, not the other way around. But, instead of propping up the husband as the dominant force in the text, Cohick says Paul has called the husband to "do those things normally reserved for the 'lesser' member of the pair. Paul describes Jesus doing 'women's work' in feeding, nurturing, making clothes, washing clothes, all in service to his bride, the church. The implicit analogy is that the husband is to do the same for his wife, who is his body." The social order is upended, and an emphasis is again placed on the love of Christ for the church and on the way that followers of Christ are called and expected to embody that love in the world, even in their marriages.

The point of Ephesians 5, then, is not to subjugate women as obedient wives and to prop men up as rulers; instead, it is an image of mutuality. The image is of Christ and the church—not as a subpoint but as the *main* point—sacrificing, self-giving, and loving for the sake of the other. This is the mutual posture that husbands and wives are to take toward one another because that is the posture all followers of Jesus are to take toward one another: a posture of mutuality and love.

The overarching picture we get of women from Genesis to Ephesians is that, although the world has often created a hierarchy in the home, where women are valued as less than, God created and intends something different. Women, along with men, are first and foremost called to be disciples of Jesus, and as they learn to follow Jesus well, they view one another as image bearers with unique gifts and talents who are worthy of love. The image of marriage is not of an overlord and a subject, or a leader and a follower, but an equal partnership of two people who work together with love, grace, and humility to reflect the abundant love of Christ to the world.

It is important to note that, although this chapter has talked in detail about the relationships between husbands and wives, not everyone is married, nor was everyone married at the time of Paul's letters, including Paul himself. There were a growing number of women who chose to stay unmarried in the early church, both as a testament to the new family being created through the church and also in order to devote themselves more fully to the work of Christ. We are reminded that Paul himself says in 1 Corinthians 7:8: "Now to the unmarried and the widows I say: It is good for them to stay unmarried, as I do." In the ancient *paterfamilias* culture, unmarried women often stayed in the house of their father until he died; however, we see that Paul and the early church often pushed against the idea of the *paterfamilias*. The early church, instead, often saw it as their responsibility to care for unmarried women, and unmarried women viewed it as their calling to care for the church.

We will explore the role of unmarried women in a later chapter, but it is important—following so much material about marriage and leadership in the home—for us to remember that single women and men in our churches are not deficient. They are fully disciples of Jesus who reflect Christ to us, to the church, and to the world. We would do well to view them as fully embodying the image of God. Even though they are in a different relationship structure than husbands and wives, these texts are all ultimately about our discipleship to Jesus, which includes married and single people alike. Single women and men are gifted in all the ways that the body of Christ is gifted.

QUESTIONS FOR DISCUSSION OR REFLECTION

1. When thinking about how sin corrupted the relationship between Adam and Eve, and how that corruption has carried down to us even today in relationships between men and women in the world, what might it look like to live in a society that isn't in bondage to sin in terms of the way men and women relate to one another?

2. Think back to the definition of *ezer kenegdo* as "a power equal to man." What implications does this meaning have not only for the relationship between spouses but also for the role of women and men in church leadership contexts?

3. What do you think a marriage built on mutual submission looks like? How might it reflect Jesus to the world?

4. In light of the scriptures we've explored in this chapter, how can our home lives—whether we're married or single, male or female—reflect Christ more faithfully?

SUGGESTIONS FOR FURTHER READING

Nijay K. Gupta, *Tell Her Story: How Women Led, Taught, and Ministered in the Early Church* (2023)

Lucy Peppiatt, *Rediscovering Scripture's Vision for Women: Fresh Perspectives on Disputed Texts* (2019)

2
WOMEN LEADERS IN THE OLD TESTAMENT

←→

Genesis laid the foundation for women to be viewed as equal, and Genesis is not the only place in the Old Testament where this message is made clear. There are numerous powerful women leaders in the Old Testament who prophesy, preach, teach, and advocate. There are male prophets who speak of the Holy Spirit pouring out on women and men alike, and images of the equality of men and women. While we often focus on the patriarchal nature of the Old Testament, we would be remiss if we didn't take time to hear and learn from the stories of women. These stories aren't always told as often, but they join the great story of God in a powerful way.

MIRIAM

In Exodus we find the story of Miriam: "Then Miriam the prophet, Aaron's sister, took a timbrel in her hand, and all the women followed her, with timbrels and dancing. Miriam sang to them: 'Sing to the LORD, for he is highly exalted. Both horse and driver he has hurled into the sea'" (Exodus 15:20–21).

Many of us picture Miriam as that young girl from Exodus 2—brave yet timid, hiding in the reeds by the Nile, keeping watch over the infant Moses, drifting down the river in his basket. Her story, much like that of Moses, doesn't end there in the reeds. Moses tends to get the spotlight in Exodus, yet Miriam also plays an integral part in the formational story of the children of Israel. Miriam is called a prophet in the Exodus text. She is described as ushering these newly freed sojourners in worship of the Lord and in celebration of the faithfulness of God. In short, she became the worship pastor for the children of God.

Some scholars have made the argument that Shiphrah and Puah, the midwives named in Exodus 1:15, are actually pseudonyms for Miriam and her mother, Jochebed, which would make these women who saved many Israelite children, irreparably damaging the system of slavery in the Egyptian empire, the same women who plotted to save Moses. Regardless of whether the midwives were Miriam and Jochebed, we still see once again another example of women being placed in high esteem, with power and authority to do the work of God in the world. The stories of Miriam and her mother and the midwives are subversive illustrations of power wielded by women to ensure that the lineage of the people of God continued, demonstrating that women stood up to the men who had the power and authority to commit genocide.

Despite these stories of leadership and bravery, it would be easy to discount Miriam. After all, Numbers 12 outlines a profound failure on her part that leads to seven days of leprosy. But even in this failure, God speaks to her directly:

> At once the LORD said to Moses, Aaron and Miriam, "Come out to the tent of meeting, all three of you." So the three of them went out. Then the LORD came down in a pillar of cloud; he stood at the entrance to the tent and summoned Aaron and Miriam. When the two of them stepped forward, he said, "Listen to my words: When there is a prophet among you, I, the LORD, reveal myself to them in visions, I speak to them in dreams. But this is not true of my servant Moses; he is faithful in all my house. With him I speak face to face, clearly and not in riddles; he sees the form of the LORD. Why then were you not afraid to speak against my servant Moses?"
>
> (Numbers 12:4–8)

God calls out and speaks directly to Miriam and her brothers. She is not the secondhand recipient of this message from God but is fully included in the message.

It would have been easy for God to have spoken only to Aaron and Moses, with a message to be passed on to Miriam, but God's inclusion of her seems to indicate that all three are viewed as leaders and prophets, and God chooses to speak to her directly, not through a man. This conversation is important to note because we often we see God speaking to men directly in Scripture, and that narrative fits the patriarchal culture of the time—yet God doesn't adhere to a strict patriarchal narrative.

QUESTIONS FOR DISCUSSION OR REFLECTION

1. Does it seem surprising for you to see God speaking directly to Miriam? Why or why not?

2. How hard or easy is it for you to imagine Miriam in a leadership role among the people of Israel?

3. We see her leading the people in a song of praise and celebration in Exodus, and we see her receiving discipline from God in Numbers. What kind of leadership role do you imagine Miriam to have occupied among the people of Israel?

DEBORAH

Miriam is not the only woman called a prophet in the Old Testament. In Judges 4:4, Deborah is called a prophet. She speaks with God on behalf of the Israelites, and to the Israelites on behalf of God. She is a judge, a leader of the people: "She held court under the Palm of Deborah between Ramah and Bethel in the hill country of Ephraim, and the Israelites went up to her to have their disputes decided" (Judges 4:5). Deborah wasn't someone that only women went to for advice, guidance, or to hear a word from the Lord. All of the Israelites—even military leaders—sought her guidance and wisdom.

The most detailed story we have about Deborah is when she sends for the military leader Barak because she has a word from the Lord for him: "She sent for Barak son of Abinoam from Kedesh in Naphtali and said to him, 'The LORD, the God of Israel, commands you: "Go, take with you ten thousand men of Naphtali and Zebulun and lead them up to Mount Tabor. I will lead Sisera, the commander of Jabin's army, with his chariots and his troops to the Kishon River and give him into your hands"'" (vv. 6–7). Here we see clearly that Deborah is a prophet, speaking to Barak on behalf of the Lord.

However, Barak is fearful and declares that he will not go without Deborah. She tells him that she will go with him, but that, because of his fear and request for Deborah's accompaniment, a woman will now receive credit for the military victory that will be accomplished (see v. 9). That woman ended up being Jael, who famously drove the tent peg through the head of the enemy commander while he rested in her tent, thinking she was his ally (see vv. 15–22).

This story of female courage in the face of male fear is a stark contrast to the patriarchal culture in which it is situated. In this patriarchal culture, honor, glory, and prestige are given primarily to men. Yet in this story, Deborah stands as a religious guide, civil judge, and military leader while another woman, Jael, is the victorious soldier who wins the battle.

OTHER WOMEN PROPHETS

Other women referred to as prophets in the Old Testament, with little surrounding context to give us clues about their lives, include Huldah, Noadiah, and Isaiah's wife.

The woman prophet Huldah is mentioned in 2 Kings 22 and 2 Chronicles 34. Huldah was approached by the most powerful men at the time of King Josiah, who entreated her to tell them what the book of Mosaic Law meant. Even though she is identified in these scriptures by way of whose wife she is, the king's men weren't seeking her husband, but her:

Hilkiah the priest, Ahikam, Akbor, Shaphan and Asaiah went to speak to the prophet Huldah, who was the wife of Shallum son of Tikvah, the son of Harhas, keeper of the wardrobe. She lived in Jerusalem, in the New Quarter. She said to them, "This is what the LORD, the God of Israel, says: Tell the man who sent you to me, 'This is what the LORD says . . .'"

(2 Kings 22:14–16a)

Huldah has power and authority to teach not only average, unremarkable men but also the king and his advisors about the word of the Lord. Huldah speaks with authority to the rulers of her day as a prophet for the Lord.

Nehemiah tells us briefly of another female prophet by name: "Remember Tobiah and Sanballat, my God, because of what they have done; remember also the prophet Noadiah and how she and the rest of the prophets have been trying to intimidate me" (6:14).

Isaiah's wife, whose name we don't know, is called a prophetess (Isaiah 8:3). Additionally, Junia Pokrifka tells us in her commentary on Exodus that there are certain places where the term "prophet" is rendered in the plural such the Hebrew grammar seems to include women as well as men.

Since the majority, if not all, of the Old Testament scriptures were written by men, it is plausible to conclude that there were other female prophets in ancient Israelite culture not named in the Old Testament—perhaps because the writers didn't know of them, or because the women themselves weren't the ones writing the narratives. Yet the inclusion of these few women as leaders in the Old Testament confirms the acceptance of women leaders in ancient times, and affirms the truth for us today that God can call women to lead in all ages, cultures, and eras.

QUESTIONS FOR REFLECTION OR DISCUSSION

1. Have you heard the stories before about Jael and Deborah? What do you think of them?

2. What do you think is the significance of a woman receiving credit for a military victory in a patriarchal culture?

3. What are the implications of the casual mentions of other women prophets in the Old Testament without stories attached to their names, or sometimes the mention of women prophets whose names are not even given? What does this treatment tell us about the relative normalcy of women prophets in ancient Israelite culture?

4. What are your thoughts on the theory that there may have been other women prophets in ancient Israel who weren't named in the Bible? What might be some additional reasons they didn't get named?

WOMEN LEADERS ACKNOWLEDGED BY MALE PROPHETS

The leadership roles of women in the Old Testament are not restricted to a few narratives about women prophets. The words of the male prophets also speak to the call and leadership of women. The prophet Joel is explicit when he speaks of the day of the Lord: "And afterward, I will pour out my Spirit on all people. Your sons and daughters will prophesy, your old men will dream dreams, your young men will see visions. Even on my servants, both men and women, I will pour out my Spirit in those days" (Joel 2:28–29). These words of the Lord declared by Joel paint a picture of justice and equality in whom the Holy Spirit calls in the world.

The day of the Lord was believed to be a day of justice, a day of jubilee, where the Lord would make all things right in the world. It is interesting, then, that Joel would declare that the day of the Lord would include women. It doesn't seem extraordinary in this culture to include men and sons, but it would seem extraordinary to include women and daughters. But this is truly the image that is being painted: a world of justice and jubilee must include women as prophets and as those who are filled with the Holy Spirit to do the work of the Lord. This passage in Joel was so cemented into the lives of the Israelites that Peter referenced it on the day of Pentecost in Acts 2. Peter declared, "No, this is what was spoken by the prophet Joel" (v. 16). Then he quoted Joel 2:28–32, using the prophecy to define and explain the inbreaking of the Holy Spirit into the lives of the new Christians.

In Jeremiah 9, we see another picture of women leading. In the midst of lament and grief over Israel, Jeremiah says, on behalf of God, to "call for the wailing women to come" (v. 17).

Wailing women were professional mourners who led funeral processions and showed people how to mourn. Jeremiah, still speaking for God, goes on to say, "Now, you women, hear the word of the LORD; open your ears to the words of his mouth. Teach your daughters how to wail; teach one another a lament" (v. 20). Women were expected to play an important role in lamenting Israel's destruction. They were the instructors who would pass on to new generations how to lament. It is worth noting that laments make up 70 percent of the Psalms, which means there is a significant amount of lament to be taught. Even though Jeremiah references the significant role of women in the process of lament, we acknowledge that most of the laments in Scripture were written by men, which shows that the task of learning to lament was not relegated to a single gender but was and is supposed to be shared by all who follow God. Jaime Clark-Soles even argues "that the imagery of the women in Jeremiah 9 plays a crucial role in understanding Judah's traumatic experience. The wailing women's tears, which represent the depth of the community's emotion in the face of extreme trauma, are closely connected to the tears of God in Jeremiah 8:21–22 . . . to the extent that we can say God's tears are embodied in those of the wailing women."

Women not only reflect the *image* of God, as we explored in chapter 1 through the Genesis narrative, but here in Jeremiah 9 we also see women reflecting the *heart* of God through lament over injustice. In her article about wailing women and trauma in our world, Juliana Claassens says, "Wailing women's tears became a way to resist the brutal devastation of the empire that has crushed everything in its way, by refusing to accept the current situation as it is." These women acted as prophets because they called the people to be honest with themselves about the horrors they faced, they called the people to be honest before God and before others, and they called everyone to hope that the current reality was not the way things were meant to be. Clark-Soles reminds us that the wailing women also serve as an example to us of incarnational ministry, illustrating to the suffering that God "understands their plight and cares deeply about it."

Women were a key component in helping the entire Israelite community of faith learn to lament what was wrong, repent, and find restoration with God. Akin to Miriam as the worship leader of the Israelites, these wailing women taught the people of God to worship through songs of lament.

QUESTIONS FOR DISCUSSION OR REFLECTION

1. Do you agree with the author that these references to women in Joel and in Jeremiah indicate the significance of female leadership in the ancient Israelite community? Why or why not?

2. How does learning about the wailing women in Jeremiah help you understand the role that women can play in leading a community of faith to lament?

3. How might women be uniquely gifted to help lead the church in lament?

RUTH

In addition to these leadership roles for women that we've explored in Old Testament texts, we also find in our Old Testament two books dedicated to and named for women who occupied important leadership roles in the community of ancient Israel—Ruth and Esther.

Ruth is a short story that elevates and celebrates not just a woman but a *foreign* woman, from a land the Israelites historically considered enemies. The story begins with death. Naomi and her husband moved with their two sons from Israel to Moab trying to escape a famine. In Moab, both sons married local Moabite women, one of whom was Ruth. Then all of Naomi's men—her husband and her two sons—died, leaving her and her daughters-in-law without protection or provision. Naomi decided that her only option for survival was to make the journey back to her homeland. She released both her daughters-in-law of their obligation to her, indicating that they should stay in Moab and try to remarry so they could be provided for. Ruth decided, however, to stay and journey back to Israel with Naomi. It wasn't an easy decision, and the life they began in Bethlehem was not easy either. Ruth and Naomi had no choice but to depend on the generosity of others as gleaners in the harvest fields. Yet these intelligent and resourceful women ended up creating a plan to catch the eye of Naomi's distant relative Boaz, who ultimately married Ruth, becoming a kinsman redeemer for Naomi's family line, which turned out to be important because that family line eventually produced the Messiah.

Ruth's story doesn't explicitly argue for the right of women to preach or prophesy, but it does reveal to us what life was like for women in that era and culture. In her New Beacon Bible Commentary, Sarah Derck explains that the book of Ruth also "challenges those who insist that the Bible is exclusively androcentric. Its inclusion in the [biblical] canon . . . provides internal critique of the canon's own male focus, and so invites readers to a more nuanced encounter with ancient Israel." In short, the inclusion of this book about a woman challenges our presuppositions and biases about whom Scripture is for and who gets to tell Scripture's story.

Ruth's story is challenging in numerous ways. She's an outsider in Israel and repeatedly becomes a victim of patriarchal society. The death of her husband left both her and Naomi incredibly vulnerable. In fact, Boaz told those working in his field to leave Ruth alone and allow her to work (2:15), which is an indication to us of her vulnerability. Yet the tenacity, ingenuity, bravery, and faith of both Ruth and Naomi led not only to their survival but also to their perpetuating the genealogical line of Jesus, making them ancestors of the Messiah himself; Ruth is one of only five women to be listed in the genealogy of Jesus found in Matthew 1.

Another important element to Ruth's story can be seen in the way she pursued Boaz. At times, Christians have advised young unmarried women to "wait for their Boaz," but Ruth did not wait. Ruth and Naomi developed a plan where Ruth took the initiative in pursuit of Boaz. This story is played out in Ruth 3:1–11:

> One day Ruth's mother-in-law Naomi said to her, "My daughter, I must find a home for you, where you will be well provided for. Now Boaz, with whose women you have worked, is a relative of ours. Tonight he will be winnowing barley on the threshing floor. Wash, put on perfume, and get dressed in your best clothes. Then go down to the threshing floor, but don't let him know you are there until he has finished eating and drinking. When he lies down, note the place where he is lying. Then go and uncover his feet and lie down. He will tell you what to do."
>
> "I will do whatever you say," Ruth answered. So she went down to the threshing floor and did everything her mother-in-law told her to do.
>
> When Boaz had finished eating and drinking and was in good spirits, he went over to lie down at the far end of the grain pile. Ruth approached quietly, uncovered his feet and lay down. In the middle of the night something startled the man; he turned—and there was a woman lying at his feet!
>
> "Who are you?" he asked.
>
> "I am your servant Ruth," she said. "Spread the corner of your garment over me, since you are a guardian-redeemer of our family."

"The LORD bless you, my daughter," he replied. "This kindness is greater than that which you showed earlier: You have not run after the younger men, whether rich or poor. And now, my daughter, don't be afraid. I will do for you all you ask. All the people of my town know that you are a woman of noble character."

The initiative that Ruth took with bravery and confidence led to her inclusion in the lineage of Christ, and was the salvation for Naomi and herself. She took the lead, and it turned out both for her good and for the good of the world.

Some might argue that Ruth wasn't really a leader in the sense that we might think of leadership today, yet her inclusion in the biblical narrative as the heroine of her own story, and her naming in the lineage of Jesus illustrate in profoundly important ways God's inclusivity toward women in the story of God in the world. Women were not created only to play supporting roles but are intended and expected to be active and leading participants in the story of God.

QUESTIONS FOR DISCUSSION OR REFLECTION

1. What lessons can women leaders today take from Ruth's example?

2. How does Ruth embody leadership qualities without being in a traditional or acknowledged leadership role?

3. How might Naomi also be considered a leader and role model in her community?

ESTHER

Another story that shows us a leading woman as part of God's larger work of restoration and redemption in the world is that of Esther. Esther is another book in the Old Testament that is a short story featuring a woman at the center.

The book of Esther opens with the focus not upon Esther herself but on the power of King Xerxes. Chapter 1 reveals the power and vast wealth of the king as he is engages in a full 180-day celebration of his wealth and glory. We see the extent of wealth in this first chapter, but we can also see the king's lack of self-control: "By the king's command each guest was allowed to drink with no restrictions, for the king instructed all the wine stewards to serve each man what he wished" (v. 8). Into this drunken group of men, King Xerxes called for his wife, Queen Vashti, to come.

Scholars don't all agree on what the purpose was for Xerxes to summon Queen Vashti, except for the obvious: it was yet another way to illustrate how powerful Xerxes was, and perhaps he wanted to showcase her beauty. Some think his command for her to come in her crown meant that he wanted her to appear wearing *only* her crown and that Queen Vashti's refusal to participate illustrates her tremendous bravery. Regardless of the circumstances, there is no denying that it would have been dangerous for any woman to show up in a room full of drunk, powerful men.

Vashti is not the main character of this story, yet it is important for us to note that she also acts as a powerful female leader. Even though her defiance of the king ultimately leads to her dethroning, and we don't know much about Vashti outside of this single act, this one decision, according to Elaine Bernius, is Vashti asserting "her human right to say no, to determine where, when, and under what circumstances her body may be seen." Vashti's example is a powerful one for women in any era who have been forced to give up their bodily autonomy in a world that continually others them. The reality of hardship and dehumanization for women is on full display here in the text of Esther. Bernius in The New Beacon Bible Commentary addresses the importance of Vashti's assertion of her own agency:

> The functional purpose of Xerxes' decree in [chapter 1] is to silence women and empower men in imperially sanctioned dominance. This legislated practice remains a reality for millions of women across our world today, while the func-

tional attitude is experienced by women even in free societies (and even in our churches!). A Wesleyan perspective speaks directly to this type of oppression, affirming that all humanity, male and female, are created in the image of God (Gen 1:27) and all are one in him (Gal 3:28). The effects of the curse (Gen 3:16) have been fully eradicated by the work of Jesus Christ, and this eradication can be fully realized in this world by the power of the Holy Spirit working through the lives of God's people. . . . For all Christians and hopefully for Wesleyans in particular, exposure to the violation of any person in any circumstance must stir in us unrest and spur us to the righting of wrongs and bringing of justice to this world. . . . We are compelled to hear Vashti's story with those ears and see with those eyes, even though this probably was not the author's intent.

Vashti's refusal enraged the king, and he dethroned her, which is how and why our heroine Esther, also known as Hadassah, entered the story. In this world ruled by men, the king was able to put out a search immediately for a new queen. It was not a request but rather a demand for women who were considered to be lovely. We know the king had a harem, one aspect of which involved sexual slavery. Bernius reminds us that the women who lived in the palace lived lives that were "fully devoted to the whim and pleasure of the king."

The reality was far from the romantic love story we might wish to imagine; in the palace, women were subservient to the king in all ways. Esther was brought into this world to compete with other women for the honor of becoming the new queen. The language in Esther 2 is passive when describing the women, including Esther, who competed before the king for the role of his new queen. "Many young women were brought," and, "Esther also was taken" (v. 8) are phrases that tell us none of these women had a choice. Esther hid her Jewish identity from this non-Jewish king, and she was ultimately chosen to replace Queen Vashti.

While Esther served in her new role as queen, a plot was hatched and put into action to kill the Jews. When Esther's cousin Mordecai informed her about it, she asked him what she was supposed to do about it. She had no power. Her position as queen was little more than figurative—her beauty served as a way for Xerxes to showcase his vast sexual wealth. One of the rules of the court was that Esther wasn't allowed to approach the king without first being summoned by him because, as she explained to Mordecai, "All the king's officials and the people of the royal provinces know that for any man or woman who approaches the king in the inner court without being summoned the king has but one law: that they be put to death unless the king extends the gold scepter to them and spares their lives. But thirty days have passed since I was called to go to the king" (4:11).

Mordecai had an answer ready for her, though: "Do not think that because you are in the king's house you alone of all the Jews will escape. For if you remain silent at this time, relief and deliverance for the Jews will arise from another place, but you and your father's family will perish. And who knows but that you have come to your royal position for such a time as this?" (4:13–14).

In an extreme act of bravery, Esther then went to the king and asked for deliverance for her people—and the king granted her request. Esther's leadership came in the form of a marginalized person who was given a certain measure of power and who placed all that power on the line for the sake of her people.

King Xerxes could have called for her to be dethroned just as he did to Vashti, but he didn't. God instead used Esther's voice and her courage to deliver God's people. Esther's story demonstrates God's deep care for God's people, including women, and it once again shows us that women play an important role in the grand story of God. It may take bravery to speak to power, but women are also called to do that work, to be leaders who take risks and ultimately change the world.

QUESTIONS FOR DISCUSSION OR REFLECTION

1. What about Esther's story inspires or encourages you?

2. How does Esther's story show that leadership isn't always a choice we make for ourselves?

3. God is not mentioned in the book of Esther, yet how can we see God at work anyway in Esther's story?

THE DAUGHTERS OF ZELOPHEHAD

Many of the women we've talked about in this chapter had prominent leadership roles. Whether they were thrust into the position like Esther, or they had a prophetic call like Miriam, they loom greatly in our minds. There are also lesser-known scriptures that speak to the leadership of women. One such story is nestled in the book of Numbers. Numbers is part of the Torah, the collection of books that hold all the Jewish laws, so it might seem surprising that there is a story there that lays a foundation for the leadership of women:

> The daughters of Zelophehad son of Hepher, the son of Gilead, the son of Makir, the son of Manasseh, belonged to the clans of Manasseh son of Joseph. The names of the daughters were Mahlah, Noah, Hoglah, Milkah and Tirzah. They came forward and stood before Moses, Eleazar the priest, the leaders and the whole assembly at the entrance to the tent of meeting and said, "Our father died in the wilderness. He was not among Korah's followers, who banded together against the LORD, but he died for his own sin and left no sons. Why should our father's name disappear from

his clan because he had no son? Give us property among our father's relatives."

So Moses brought their case before the LORD, and the LORD said to him, "What Zelophehad's daughters are saying is right. You must certainly give them property as an inheritance among their father's relatives and give their father's inheritance to them.

"Say to the Israelites, 'If a man dies and leaves no son, give his inheritance to his daughter. If he has no daughter, give his inheritance to his brothers. If he has no brothers, give his inheritance to his father's brothers. If his father had no brothers, give his inheritance to the nearest relative in his clan, that he may possess it. This is to have the force of law for the Israelites, as the LORD commanded Moses.'"
(Numbers 27:1–11)

The daughters of Zelophehad did something leaders do: they advocated for themselves before Moses and the other leaders so they would get the inheritance of their father. This story might seem insignificant to those who live in a culture where it is customary to leave inheritance to daughters and sons alike, but prior to this advocacy, daughters were not given an inheritance from their parents. The outcome of this story set the groundwork for women to own property and share in the generational wealth of their families. Women were to be viewed equally as far as inheritance and property were concerned. According to Numbers 5:6–7, they were also supposed to be punished equally for wrongdoing. This story in Numbers is yet another illustration that God's intent for humanity from the beginning was to exist as equals in the world.

The Old Testament is often accused of being archaic, outdated, or simply lacking in its treatment of women, and it is important to acknowledge that there are some incredibly troubling passages, but these stories of powerful women and the evidence they give us of the continued call of God to participate in God's greater story are a profound message for us even now.

There is a powerful verse in Psalm 68:11: "The Lord announces the word, and the women who proclaim it are a mighty throng." There are numerous versions of Scripture that translate this passage without the feminine wording, but the Hebrew word used here is feminine, giving us an image of a large number of women proclaiming the word of the Lord. Another word for proclaiming the word of the Lord is preaching. The psalmist is painting a beautiful image—much like Joel when he says daughters will prophesy—of a great number of women preaching the good news of the kingdom of God.

Perhaps the psalmist had heard the stories of many of the women leaders who preceded him. Maybe he had heard of the daughters of Zelophehad, of Deborah and Jael, of Eve being created in the image of God as a power equal to men, and therefore knew that God was using women to participate in telling God's great story. Perhaps the psalmist also had in mind the women who would come after him, maybe even the women who were to usher in the good news of the coming Messiah. Maybe, in the way that only the Holy Spirit can do, the psalmist was given an image of all of these women from the past, the present, and the future declaring the mighty word of the Lord, a great many together, a powerful and resounding throng.

QUESTIONS FOR DISCUSSION OR REFLECTION

1. Which of the women discussed in this chapter was the most unknown to you previously? What did you learn about her, and what stood out the most about her story?

2. What do you think the word "prophet" means? Have you ever imagined a woman occupying the role of a prophet? What do you think Joel meant when he said "your sons and daughters will prophesy"?

3. What places in this chapter challenged what you have previously believed about the Old Testament, or about women?

4. What do you think the psalmist meant when he painted the image of the women proclaiming the word of the Lord in a "mighty throng" in Psalm 68:11? What image do you see when you read that verse?

SUGGESTIONS FOR FURTHER READING

Jaime Clark-Soles, *Women in the Bible: Resources for the Use of Scripture in the Church* (2020)

Sarah B. C. Derck, Joseph Coleson, and Elaine Bernius, *Ruth, Song of Songs, Esther,* New Beacon Bible Commentary (2020)

H. Junia Pokrifka, *Exodus,* New Beacon Bible Commentary (2018)

3
WOMEN AND JESUS

←——→

As we turn the page to the New Testament, we are welcomed into the story of salvation through Jesus. Jesus is the central figure of the New Testament and the gospel story. He is God incarnate in the world, and as followers of Christ, he is the one around whom our lives are oriented; therefore, examining how Jesus interacted with and related to women is important for those who seek to be disciples of Jesus.

What we find when we dive in is that Jesus valued and cared for women deeply. He befriended women, he had disciples who were women, he listened to women, he sent women out to declare good news, and he even debated and was corrected by women. The numerous stories of how Jesus related to women give us insight into God's desire for women leaders in the world.

MARY MAGDALENE

On the first day of the week, very early in the morning, the women took the spices they had prepared and went to the tomb. They found the stone rolled away from the tomb, but when they entered, they did not find the body of the Lord Jesus. While they were wondering about this, suddenly two men in clothes that gleamed like lightning stood beside them. In their fright the women bowed down with their faces to the ground, but the men said to them, "Why do you look for the living among the dead? He is not here; he has risen! Remember how he told you, while he was still with you in Galilee: 'The Son of Man must be delivered over to the hands of sinners, be crucified and on the third day be raised again.'" Then they remembered his words.

When they came back from the tomb, they told all these things to the Eleven and to all the others. It was Mary Magdalene, Joanna, Mary the mother of James, and the others with them who told this to the apostles. But they did not believe the women, because their words seemed to them like nonsense.
(Luke 24:1–11)

Each of the Gospel narratives—Matthew, Mark, Luke, and John—contains its own account of Jesus's death and resurrection, and in each one, women were present. Although the Gospels vary in their recounting of who was present at the empty tomb on that first Easter morning, there is consistency among all four in the naming of Mary Magdalene. In the Gospel of John, she is the only named person: "Early on the first day of the week, while it was still dark, Mary Magdalene went to the tomb and saw that the stone had been removed from the entrance" (John 20:1).

Mary Magdalene is an important figure in the New Testament texts. Because of her presence on that first Easter Sunday, and because of her subsequent sharing of the news of the empty tomb, she has been referred to as "the apostle to the apostles." It was not a man who first shared the good news of Jesus's resurrection—it was this woman, and potentially other women who were with her.

Mary Magdalene is also the first named in the lists of women in both Mark 15 and Luke 8, and according to Joan E. Taylor and Helen Bond in the book *Women Remembered*, she is mentioned more in the Gospels and other early Christian literature than any other women, except for Jesus's mother. The significance of her being the first named indicates that she was likely viewed as highly important among the female disciples and that her name was widely known, which illustrates her prominence and importance as a disciple of Christ.

What do *we* know about Mary Magdalene, and what does that mean for women in leadership in the church? The most obvious thing to note about Mary Magdalene is her name. Mary was the most common female name at the time, so her identification as Magdalene helps differentiate her from other Marys. Many scholars believe that "Magdalene" was used because she was from a place called Magdala. However, not everyone agrees on the origin of "Magdalene" to differentiate this Mary from other ancient Marys. Taylor and Bond share that fourth-century Christian scholar Jerome said, "Mary was not named 'the Magdalene' after a place; she was so-named because of her outstanding faith. The word Magdalaitha, in Aramaic . . . translates as 'the tower-ess' or 'she who was made great' or 'the aggrandised/ magnified one.'" If Jerome is correct, then it is clear that Mary Magdalene was regarded with high esteem as a disciple of Jesus since the days of the early church.

Although we can't fully know the extent of Mary's discipleship with Jesus, we can be confident that she was present on Easter, and that she was entrusted with the task of sharing the news of Jesus's resurrection with the disciples—and the world. She was clearly dedicated to following Christ wherever he led. Even when the men were afraid, she was present, following Christ.

Mary Magdalene was the first person to speak the words, "We have seen the Lord!" These words are the first testimony to the resurrection, a testimony we still reference each Easter in our churches today, illustrating its enduring power. Some have argued that women's testimonies were not admissible in a court of law in the ancient world, and others have posited that Mary's preaching was limited, meant only as a message to the male disciples, who would then surpass her in the important task of carrying the gospel message to the rest of the world. Yet, as Lucy Peppiatt reminds us, the Gospel writers themselves clearly note that the women made this first resurrection testimony, and their honest recording of the men's initial refusal to believe them is also clear in Scripture, to their own shame.

QUESTIONS FOR DISCUSSION OR REFLECTION

1. What associations did you have with the character of Mary Magdalene before reading this section?

2. What is the significance of Jesus entrusting the resurrection testimony to women in an age and culture when women were not considered trustworthy witnesses?

ELIZABETH AND MARY THE MOTHER OF JESUS

Mary Magdalene's declaration of the resurrection is evidence of a woman preaching and declaring the gospel message, but she isn't the only woman in Scripture to declare the presence of the Messiah. Before Jesus was even born, we see two women taking active roles in ushering in the message of the Messiah: Elizabeth and Mary the mother of Jesus.

Elizabeth played a prominent prophetic role in announcing the coming of the Messiah. We find her story in Luke 1, starting with the recounting of her own miraculous pregnancy with the child who would become the figure we now know as John the Baptist. In this story, Zechariah—Elizabeth's husband and a respected priest—was rendered mute by an angel of God due to his unbelief. In a story of this nature, Zechariah's voice would normally be the one people expected to hear. He was the authority of the household in this culture, after all: he was the husband, the father-to-be, and a religious leader. Yet the dominant voice in this narrative belonged to a woman.

While they were both pregnant, Elizabeth and Mary had a visit together, during which Elizabeth became the first person to declare Jesus as Lord: "When Elizabeth heard Mary's greeting, the baby leaped in her womb, and Elizabeth was filled with the Holy Spirit. In a loud voice she exclaimed: 'Blessed are you among women, and blessed is the child you will bear! But why am I so favored, that the mother of my Lord should come to me?'" (Luke 1:41–43). Elizabeth declared *in a loud voice* that the unborn Jesus was Lord. She interpreted the movement of her own unborn child, taking it to mean that Mary's pregnancy was a significant one. This is the work of a prophet. Elizabeth was not a silent and meek woman but a loud and confident announcer of the coming of the Lord—just as her son, John the Baptist, would eventually also be.

When her own son was born, Elizabeth stepped into a leadership role once again: "On the eighth day they came to circumcise the child, and they were going to name him after his father Zechariah, but his mother spoke up and said, 'No! He is to be called John'" (Luke 1:59–60). Despite societal pressure to do otherwise, Elizabeth named her son John in obedience to the message from the angel (v. 13). Once again, Elizabeth was not silent, even during this sacred religious ceremony. She spoke confidently, a loud declaration of truth in a space likely filled with both men and women, religious leaders and laypeople alike.

Like Elizabeth, Mary the mother of Jesus was a woman who spoke up and took on a prophetic role of leadership. Perhaps because of images we have seen in religious art or nativity scenes, we might imagine Mary to be quiet and docile, but Scripture doesn't seem to paint her that way at all. Luke 1 centers Mary as a woman who spoke up—or rather sang—boldly and authoritatively about the coming Messiah. The angel Gabriel announced to Mary that she would bear the Messiah (vv. 31–33). Although Mary would certainly have been aware of the stigma and consequences surrounding her pregnancy as an unwed woman, she still submitted in obedience to doing what God asked of her. She made a bold choice, not a weak one, to trust God in spite of the inevitable trials that would come.

Her bold strength was demonstrated again when Mary took on the role of a biblical scholar and prophet in the song she sang while visiting Elizabeth (vv. 46–55). This passage of scripture, known as the *Magnificat*, is a strong prophetic declaration about who Jesus was going to be. It also references numerous Old Testament scriptures. It is patterned after Hannah's prayer in 1 Samuel 2, references the song of Deborah in Judges 5, and also alludes to the song of Miriam in Exodus 15. The *Magnificat* contains many other Old Testament references—with scholars saying as many as thirty-five or more. The depth of Mary's understanding of Scripture was profound, and she sang with the authority to interpret that Scripture for her current situation. Bible scholar Jaime Clark-Soles says of the significance of Mary's song: "Mary exhibits the passion of the prophets and conveys God's preferential option for the poor. She draws upon her Scriptures (the notes in any good scholarly study Bible will show you the variety of texts she includes), and she announces Luke's primary theme, the great reversal. . . . The high are brought low, the lowly exalted. Those marginalized in this world are the apple of God's eye."

As Jesus grew, Mary continued to speak up. In John 2, Mary was the one who initiated Jesus's miracle of turning water into wine by telling Jesus about the problem. Jesus even argued with her that it wasn't his time yet, but he ultimately submitted to the request of his mother.

So often, we only imagine Mary as the young mother giving birth in the stable, yet Mary shows up throughout the New Testament, beyond the familiar stories about her pregnancy, her marriage to Joseph, and her giving birth to Jesus. Mary can also be found in: Luke 2, at the temple; John 2, at the wedding in Cana; Mark 3, when there was hostility toward Jesus in Capernaum; Mark 6, when Jesus was rejected by his own village; Mark 15 and John 19, at the foot of the cross while Jesus was crucified; Acts 1, at Pentecost; and various other New Testament texts where she is mentioned or where Jesus mentions mothers in a way that could point to Mary. Mary is prominent throughout the New Testament, always affirming that Christ came, that Christ died, and that Christ rose again. She knew—because she was there for all of it.

QUESTIONS FOR DISCUSSION OR REFLECTION

1. What does it mean for Elizabeth to have made prophetic statements about Jesus while Mary was pregnant?

2. John the Baptist is well known to us as a prophet whose entire purpose was to point to the coming of Jesus. What new significance does his role gain when we see that his own mother spoke prophetic words over Jesus in Mary's womb before John and Jesus were even born?

3. How important was it for Elizabeth to be the one who declared that her child would be called John and not Zechariah after his father?

4. How have you imagined Mary before now? Did you ever think about her role beyond giving birth to Jesus?

5. What is prophetic about Mary's role in the Bible? Where does she show leadership?

ANNA

Anna was another female prophet who showed up early in Jesus's life. Her story can be found in Luke 2. Like the women in the Old Testament who were called prophets, that is the word used for Anna as well. Although Anna's story takes place in a relatively short text, we learn a lot about her in just a couple of verses: she was old, her husband died when they had only been married for seven years, she never remarried, and she never left the temple but remained there worshiping, praying, and fasting day and night.

What happened in verse 38 can be overlooked easily, but it is important: "Coming up to them [Mary, Joseph, and the child Jesus] at that very moment, she gave thanks to God and spoke about the child to all who were looking forward to the redemption of Jerusalem." Anna pointed to Jesus as the hope for Jerusalem's redemption! Since Anna spent her days and nights at the temple, it is safe to assume she interacted regularly with people who longed for the Messiah. After this encounter with the Christ child, Anna probably spent the rest of her life, however long or short it was, sharing the good news about Jesus.

Jaime Clark-Soles says this about Anna: "Her life just doesn't seem that impressive, and you might feel sorry for her or expect her to feel sorry for herself. Such an assessment ignores Luke's message about the nature of the kingdom of God, who figures prominently in it, and what matters. . . . Anna understands which world is real. It is not the world obsessed with superficial happiness, staying young, staying healthy, 'having it all': the real world is God's kingdom." Anna is an example not only of how God uses women to prophesy and preach good news but also of how God uses women of various ages, stages of life, and from different circumstances. We are never too old (or too young!) to be used by God.

QUESTIONS FOR DISCUSSION OR REFLECTION

1. If Anna never remarried and never left the temple, what does that tell you about her relationship with God?

2. Would Anna's reputation at the temple have made her a trustworthy source of prophecy, or do you think her words would've been received with skepticism?

THE WOMAN AT THE WELL

God uses women from various cultural, ethnic, and social backgrounds to lead. Quite possibly the most profound example of this diversity is the Samaritan woman at the well in John 4. Before we dive too deeply into her story as a leader, Clark-Soles offers us an important reminder that "nowhere is this woman referred to as a 'whore' (*pornē*), and nowhere is she forgiven (*aphiemi*). . . . The reader focused on the woman's sexual history misses out on what the story is *actually* about—an exemplar of the faith whom the reader is supposed to imitate."

The Samaritan woman who interacted with Jesus at the well in the middle of the day has been maligned by commentators throughout history who have taken a couple of individual verses out of historical and textual context:

"I have no husband," she replied.

Jesus said to her, "You are right when you say you have no husband. The fact is, you have had five husbands, and the man you now have is not your husband. What you have just said is quite true."
(John 4:17–18)

In his commentary on the Gospel of John, New Testament scholar Scot McKnight says,

"Why would a woman have five husbands and now a man who is not her husband? Anyone who knows Judaism can think of more than the sexually promiscuous or immoral-woman view. Her husbands could have died. . . . She could have been passed around through the laws of levirate marriage in which, if a man died, his brother took his sister-in-law under his own care. . . . She could have been divorced a time or two, perhaps especially if she was a barren woman. . . . She could be said to 'have' a man, and the word could mean nothing more than 'man' and not 'husband,' because she is a concubine of a Roman leader who could not marry a woman of a lower class. Committed cohabitation was a known institution in that world too. Or, more likely, she was under the care of her brother, her former husband's brother, or an uncle. Such explanations are not only possible but should be our first instincts.

John 4 is one of those texts where it's important for us to take the time to read the actual text ourselves. Often we assume some detail or other is in the text because we've heard a sermon or another message about it without looking at the text itself. John 4 is also one of the many places in Scripture that needs some cultural understanding to bridge the contextual gap between the ancient setting of the story and our world today.

Because we have often viewed this woman through the lens of promiscuity—something that isn't actually overtly present in the passage—we have missed the depth of her conversation with Jesus about living water, and we may also have missed this key conclusion to the story: "Many of the Samaritans from that town believed in him because of the woman's testimony" (John 4:39). This woman declared the gospel of Jesus to her entire town, and many of them believed because of her. She was a leader whom the people of her town followed and who was considered trustworthy enough that, when she shared with them about who Jesus was, they believed her.

A Samaritan woman became a leader who transformed an entire community because of her faithfulness to Jesus and to his message. In doing so, she has become a model disciple for all of us. The woman at the well illustrates for us once again that God raises up leaders from unexpected places and circumstances to share the good news. Regardless of her background, the Samaritan woman was a disciple of Jesus and a leader for a community that was forever changed because of her.

QUESTIONS FOR DISCUSSION OR REFLECTION

1. What lesson can we learn from the story of the woman at the well and the unwarranted assumptions that have been made about her by biblical scholars throughout history?

2. Read John 4:27. What strikes you about this verse and about the disciples' reaction to finding Jesus and this woman in conversation?

UNNAMED/IMPLIED WOMEN

Over and over again, like with the Samaritan woman, we see Jesus send out women to share the good news of Christ with the world, and we see it again in a more obscure text: "Calling the Twelve to him, he began to send them out two by two and gave them authority over impure spirits" (Mark 6:7). The language "two by two" in the Greek is translated the same as the Hebrew phrase "two by two" in Genesis 6 and 7, used to describe the male-female pairs of animals that Noah was instructed to take onto the ark. Scholar Joan E. Taylor has done a thorough word study on the Greek term for "two by two" and finds reason to conclude that, even though women disciples are not overtly evident in the Gospel of Mark, "it is likely that some [of the original audience] at least imagined female partners of the named male apostles, not pairings within a group of twelve men."

This conclusion makes sense given the cultural structures in place at the time. Women and men often took up different spaces. In order to share the message of Jesus with the most people, having both a woman and a man sent to do that work as a team would make logical sense. For example, a man would be able to enter all-male spaces, like the temple, where a woman might not be welcome. Likewise, a woman would be able to enter certain marketplace spaces dominated by women, or be welcomed into homes in a way that would have seemed improper for men. Having male and female ministry pairs would have allowed the good news to be shared in more places and spaces than if a single-gender pair were sent.

Sending male-female teams of disciples into the world to share good news also fits the broader narrative of Scripture, as we have already seen, and will continue to see in our study. This type of ministry pairing happens in the letters of Paul as well, with married couples like Priscilla and Aquila, so it makes sense to conclude that these pairings were already happening within Jesus's ministry.

THE CANAANITE WOMAN

Jesus also had theological discussions with women, like the Canaanite woman in Matthew 15 (referred to as the Syrophoenician woman in Mark's version of the story). The story says the Canaanite woman had a daughter suffering greatly from demon possession. She went to Jesus in desperation, but she was an outsider. She was not a Jewish woman, so Jesus's response is often received harshly by audiences today: "I was sent only to the lost sheep of Israel" (Matthew 15:24). However, when we look more closely at the text, it seems that the disciples were the ones treating her harshly. They wanted her sent away, without ever interacting with her—but Jesus addressed her directly.

When we look at Jesus's replies to her in the larger context of Jesus's posture of inclusivity and love throughout the Gospels, we realize the likelihood that Jesus was interacting with her from a place of compassion. He then engaged in a theological dialogue with her. In verse 26, he told her that it wasn't right to take the children's bread and feed it to the dogs.

The woman, who comes off in this passage as both intelligent and desperate, pushed back and said that even dogs get crumbs.

Jesus did not dismiss her after that comment. He didn't chastise her for speaking out of turn, or for "talking back," as though women shouldn't be speaking, or as if theology were a field of discussion women shouldn't occupy. He didn't reject her thoughts either. Instead, Jesus applauded her faith and healed her daughter.

This story stands out in significant ways because this woman was an outsider yet is portrayed in the text as a model disciple. She did what she needed to do to advocate for her daughter, even taking on a theological debate with Jesus himself. And when she challenged him, Jesus didn't condemn her but agreed with her. The Canaanite woman may not have been a religious leader or preacher, but she certainly had a strong voice, wit, and admirable theological prowess, for which Jesus praised and rewarded her.

THE BLEEDING WOMAN

One story that clearly demonstrates Jesus's love is when he cared for the woman with the issue of blood, found in Matthew 9, Mark 5, and Luke 8. This woman, like the Canaanite woman, was desperate for healing. Despite her ceremonial uncleanness, she reached out to Jesus in the middle of a crowd and was met not with rejection or disgust but with compassion. The story portrays the woman as someone with great faith, again holding her up as a model disciple.

It's also important for us to conclude that this story would've spawned a testimony for the woman. She obviously had to tell people about her healing for anyone to know she had been healed, which means people took her testimony seriously and believed her.

QUESTIONS FOR DISCUSSION OR REFLECTION

1. What are your thoughts on the idea that the disciples being sent out in pairs to do ministry could reasonably be assumed to have been male-female pairs?

2. What is your take on the story of Jesus's dialogue with the Canaanite woman? Does Jesus seem harsh to you? Does the woman seem disrespectful or impertinent with Jesus? How can this story be interpreted as Jesus having compassion on her, even before he granted her request for healing for her daughter?

3. Read Mark 5:27–32. Why do you think Jesus was so insistent on knowing who had touched him?

MARY AND MARTHA

The Bible shows us again and again that Jesus cared deeply about women, saw them as worthy of his time, and valued their opinions and thoughts. In Luke 10, we find a story of Jesus being welcomed into the home of Martha. At times this story is interpreted as two sisters pitted against each other, but when we examine the text a bit more closely, a few things are illuminated for us.

One of the first things to note in the text is verse 38: "As Jesus and his disciples were on their way, he came to a village where a woman named Martha opened her home to him." There is no mention of a husband or father. This was *Martha's* home. We often assume that women couldn't or wouldn't have owned their own property, but scholar Susan Hylen says that, in fact, "Women owned a good deal of property in the Imperial period. By some scholarly estimates they controlled one-fifth to one-third of property in the Roman Empire. Literary sources provide evidence of extremely wealthy women who own large estates. Papyrus records show non-elite women with more modest holdings, including household utensils, livestock, and farmland." Later, in Paul's letters and in early church history, women acted as benefactors and often served as leaders of house churches, in part due to the reality that they owned their own property.

Martha and her sister, Mary, appear on their own in the stories where they encounter Jesus. We know they had a brother (the famous Lazarus), but no husbands are ever mentioned, which could mean they were widows or that neither of them ever got married. Either way, this passage shows them acting independently of men.

In her sister's house, Mary chose to sit "at the Lord's feet listening to what he said" (Luke 10:39). This is the posture of a disciple. She was learning from Jesus, alongside the male disciples, seemingly without any sort of permission from any male figure. She assumed the posture of a disciple, and Jesus not only welcomed her learning, but he called it "better" in verse 42.

While Mary *learned* as a disciple, Martha *served* as one. Joan Taylor and Helen Bond point out that "it might come as a surprise to those familiar with this story to realise that food and cooking aren't actually mentioned. In the Greek, Martha is distracted with much 'serving'. The important word . . . is *diakoneo*, related to the word 'deacon' (*diakonos*). While it can mean 'waiting at tables', it can also mean rendering service and support in all kinds of ways, and when used of a man it's more commonly translated as 'ministry'." Later in Scripture the word *diakonos* is used to refer to ministry and proclamation of the gospel.

It would seem, then, both Martha and Mary were acting as disciples. Jesus pointing out to Martha that Mary chose the better way did not indicate that Martha was doing something wrong; rather it seems he was saying, "Listen first, serve later."

This same Mary's discipleship is also on display in John 12, when she anointed Jesus with a jar of nard, which was very likely to be from Mary's own money—something she herself owned. When Judas reacted negatively to the waste, Jesus praised her, indicating that she understood more about Jesus's purpose and where he was headed than his male disciples did (see vv. 7–8).

QUESTIONS FOR DISCUSSION OR REFLECTION

1. How have you interpreted Mary and Martha's story in the past, and how does this new perspective change your view of their roles in the story?

2. What is the significance of Jesus publicly praising women when others around him are trying to cut them down?

GOD ORDAINS WOMEN

When we look at Jesus's ministry to and with women we see that, as Lucy Peppiatt puts it, his "interactions and friendships with women were unqualifiedly affirming." Peppiatt goes on to say,

> A woman should feel confident to proceed in any form of ministry or service in the church simply on the basis of Jesus's treatment of women and the promise of the pouring

out of the Spirit "on all flesh," empowering the people of God for works of service. A Christ-centered (Christocentric) and Spirit-centered (pneumatocentric) approach to identity and calling should be an adequate foundation for a woman to function in all or any gifts, including pastoring, leading, and teaching. Jesus commands his disciples to make disciples of all nations. Thankfully, this command stands over the entire church and not just over men, who make up less than half of the entire body.

Wesleyan-Holiness people believe in the words and work of Jesus as God the Son, and in the power of the Holy Spirit in the lives of all believers. Taking seriously the various ways that Jesus and the Holy Spirit empower women is enough to lead us to conclude that women belong at the leadership table. Jesus commissioned women to preach the gospel, held them up as model disciples, treated them with compassion, and accepted their gifts of ministry. Women prophesied about him and were treated well by him. Women today are expected to serve in ministry and leadership roles in the same way they did during Jesus's life.

QUESTIONS FOR DISCUSSION OR REFLECTION

1. Which of the women's stories from this chapter stands out to you the most, and why?

2. What was illuminated for you in this chapter about the way Jesus interacted with women?

3. What did you find in this chapter that contradicts what you've previously heard or understood about the role of women in the Bible during the time of Jesus? How has your perspective changed?

4. Which of the women discussed in this chapter are you most interested to learn more about? How do you see yourself in the stories of these women?

SUGGESTIONS FOR FURTHER READING

Susan Hylen, *A Modest Apostle: Thecla and the History of Women in the Early Church* (2015)

Joan Taylor and Helen Bond, *Women Remembered: Jesus's Female Disciples* (2022)

Joan Taylor and Ilaria Ramelli (editors), *Patterns of Women's Leadership in Early Christianity* (2021)

4
WOMEN IN THE EARLY CHURCH

←→

Jesus's treatment of women ought to be enough for Christ followers to support women in leadership in all areas, but those who want further support can find it in the early church.

PENTECOST

The obvious first place to look is in Acts, which relates the events surrounding the day of Pentecost, which is also known as the birthday of the church.

> Then the apostles returned to Jerusalem from the hill called the Mount of Olives, a Sabbath day's walk from the city. When they arrived, they went upstairs to the room where they were staying. Those present were Peter, John, James and Andrew; Philip and Thomas, Bartholomew and Matthew; James son of Alphaeus and Simon the Zealot, and Judas son of James. They all joined together constantly in prayer, *along with the women and Mary the mother of Jesus*, and with his brothers.
> (Acts 1:12–14, emphasis added)

When we think and talk about the day of Pentecost in Acts, we often imagine a group of men gathered together in a room, but the text explicitly mentions that women, including Jesus's own mother, were also present in the room.

This detail that is often overlooked becomes important when we get to the more familiar events in Acts 2: "When the day of Pentecost came, they were all together in one place. Suddenly a sound like the blowing of a violent wind came from heaven and filled the whole house where they were sitting. They saw what seemed to be tongues of fire that separated and came to rest on each of them. All of them were filled with the Holy Spirit and began to speak in other tongues as the Spirit enabled them" (vv. 1–4). Although the presence of Mary and the other women seems less obvious in Acts 2, the language is similar, and the tradition of the early church assumes they were all still gathered together in that space—which means the Holy Spirit came upon men and women in an egalitarian way. There weren't stages to the gifting of the Spirit, where men received it first and then dispensed it to the women. Rather, the text indicates that everyone present received the gift of the Spirit at the same time and that their giftings in that moment were the same: they all began to speak in other languages. This event is explained more fully when Peter stands up and quotes the prophet Joel:

> In the last days, God says, I will pour out my Spirit on all people. Your sons and daughters will prophesy, your young men will see visions, your old men will dream dreams. Even on my servants, both men and women, I will pour out my Spirit in those days, and they will prophesy. I will show wonders in the heavens above and signs on the earth below, blood and fire and billows of smoke. The sun will be turned

to darkness and the moon to blood before the coming of the great and glorious day of the Lord. And everyone who calls on the name of the Lord will be saved.

(Acts 2:17–21)

We looked at this passage from Joel a bit when we explored women leaders in the Old Testament, but we see Peter looking at these words in a new way, claiming that this is the moment that men and women have been gifted the Spirit. Both men and women will prophesy, and indeed are already prophesying. It is a powerful statement in a patriarchal world that women are gifted the Spirit in the same way men are and that both are gifted to prophesy. The emphasis on "sons and daughters," "men and women," is significant. Women are empowered to do the work of the church, and women are sent out to do the work of the church, in the same way that men are—by the power of the Holy Spirit.

The power of the Spirit that broke through at Pentecost is the same power that is continually breaking through in our world. The reign of God is breaking into our world on earth as it is in heaven, and some of the evidence for that inbreaking is that daughters are proclaiming the good news of the Lord to the church and the world.

QUESTIONS FOR DISCUSSION OR REFLECTION

1. Have you noticed the presence of women at Pentecost in the Acts text before?

2. What does it communicate to us about women that the Holy Spirit was given to all equally?

WIDOWS

As we continue to journey through the New Testament and examine the leadership structures of the early church, we see that women took the power and indwelling of the Spirit seriously, and they did go out to do the work of the church alongside the men.

This brand-new church looked incredibly countercultural to the world in the ways that men and women worked and served. In Acts 6, the disciples were tasked with the distribution of food among the widows. Some of the widows were being overlooked—presumably because of their ethnic background. "So the Twelve gathered all the disciples together and said, 'It would not be right for us to neglect the ministry of the word of God in order to wait on tables. Brothers and sisters, choose seven men from among you who are known to be full of the Spirit and wisdom. We will turn this responsibility over to them and will give our attention to prayer and the ministry of the word'" (vv. 2–4). It stands out that this task was given to both male and female disciples to decide. They were to work together to make the decision. From this example we can conclude that the decisions of the church were not to be unilaterally decided by a team of men but were expected to be made with everyone having a voice together.

Together they were to choose seven men to do the work of passing out food to the widows in a fair distribution process. The reason this detail stands out is that serving food was generally a task for women and/or the enslaved. Even here, in this often overlooked story, the disciples seem to be making a statement that in the kingdom of God there are not lesser tasks, and even those with more social significance (in this case, men) are to become servants of all.

We also need to note the term "widow" in the text. We think of widows as solely being wives of deceased husbands, but this wasn't the case in the early church. Joan Taylor and Helen Bond point out that "the term 'widows' in the early church doesn't just mean divorced or bereaved women who were dependent on the community for support. Being a 'widow' (*chera*) was actually a designated ministry role. . . . The widows had their own *diakonia*, which involved caring for people in the community and teaching women." *Diakonia* is an important word that will continue to show up in the New Testament texts we are exploring. It is connected to the word "servant," and often pertains to work; however, it became redefined in the church. Because it was believed that Christians were to be servants of all, *diakonia* and its variations came to be the root for the English word "deacon," meaning a leader in the church. *Diakonia* is defined as the work of ministry.

Taylor and Bond go on to point out that multiple ancient church fathers talked about widows in this way. Tertullian, in the early third century, spoke of widows as being interpreters of prophecy, and indicated that they were seated along with the overseers, elders, and deacons when the church met. Origen understood that widows had ministerial roles, including being elders, and the *Testamentum of Domini* from the fifth century states that widows had oversight over female deacons and presbyters in the same way that bishops had oversight over male deacons. It goes on to say that widows were ordained and seated next to the bishop.

This order of widows is evident in Acts 9 when we are introduced to the disciple Tabitha (or Dorcas). Although Tabitha's story in Acts focuses on the fact that she was miraculously raised from the dead, it's important to note that she is referred to as a "disciple" (v. 36). Some point to the fact that Jesus's twelve disciples were all men as proof that women cannot also be disciples, yet we already explored the way Jesus himself included women as disciples, and Tabitha's story is yet more evidence that women were and are considered disciples. Tabitha is also described as a woman who "was always doing good and helping the poor" (v. 36). This description implies what we know about the word *diakanos*—that she was doing ministry work.

We see further evidence of Tabitha's contribution to ministry and to her community in verse 39: "Peter went with them, and when he arrived he was taken upstairs to the room. All the widows stood around him, crying and showing him the robes and other clothing that Dorcas had made while she was still with them." Tabitha was actively engaged in the work of caring for others, and she was viewed as a disciple and valuable contributor to the Christian community she was part of. As someone in this order of widows, she would also have been viewed as a leader in the church.

These widows not only help us to see that women were viewed as leaders within the early church, but they also cause us to recognize how valued single women were. We often can assume there was no place for single women in the church and that they had no power or rights without a husband. Although we acknowledge the reality that it was a patriarchal society, and we don't want to deny the challenges that reality created for women, there is still evidence of wealthy women wielding power of their own, often in the form of status. And, since there wasn't language for unmarried women who reached a certain age, these women joined the work of the church in the orders of widows. They were well respected and did important work, and they serve as a reminder for all of us that single women are not exempt from leadership within the church, and haven't been since its earliest days.

QUESTIONS FOR DISCUSSION OR REFLECTION

1. What do you think about the "order of widows" idea introduced in this section? What are your thoughts about a group that seems to have been its own ministry team with designated ministry tasks, and included divorced women and women who had never been married in addition to women whose husbands had died?

2. Now that we know Tabitha was called a disciple and was part of the order of widows who engaged in ministry, what might we interpret from verse 39, where the other widows showed Peter all the things Tabitha made? Why might she have made so many pieces of clothing, and why would the other widows have wanted Peter to see them?

PRISCA

Prisca, or Priscilla, is another prominent female leader we first learn about in Acts 18. The name Priscilla is a variation of the more formal and common name Prisca. Priscilla literally means "little Prisca." Priscilla was generally used as a nickname, so when referring to this biblical character, scholars often use the more formal variation of the name because it was the one more commonly used at the time. The fact that the nickname Priscilla is the one we see used in Scripture may reveal the closeness of the relationship the writer of Acts had with Prisca.

When we first meet Prisca, we learn that she and her husband, Aquila, fled Rome and settled as tentmakers in Corinth. Paul was a tentmaker as well, so it's possible that's how he came to know this couple. Paul then took Prisca and Aquila with him to be missionaries in Ephesus. Clearly Paul viewed this pair as his ministry coworkers and wanted them to be involved in the establishment of the church in Ephesus.

Interestingly, in Acts 18:19, Prisca is listed first when she and her husband are named. This order is repeated again in Romans 16:3. Scholar Ilaria Ramelli tells us that this ordering of the names "suggests that Prisca, not Aquila, was the leading member, and key host, who can be considered to have presided over a house church and to have celebrated the Eucharist there." Ramelli emphasizes this point again when noting, "Prisca in Pauline texts and Acts is shown to be a wife equal to her husband as a missionary."

In Acts 18:26, Prisca is again the first listed when the pair are teaching Apollos more thoroughly about the ways of Jesus, suggesting that she took the lead in teaching Apollos. Prisca wasn't someone who was merely along for the ride, or brought solely to teach the women but is seen in Acts 18:26 teaching a man. Prisca was not a minor character in the early church but a missionary, a teacher, and a leader.

Although Prisca and Aquila did important work in Ephesus, they didn't stay there. We find them mentioned again in Romans 16, where we see that Prisca became involved in the establishment of the church in Rome.

Romans 16 reads a bit like a Who's Who in the early church in Rome, and that list includes a great number of other women, in addition to Prisca, for us to learn about.

I commend to you our sister Phoebe, a deacon of the church in Cenchreae. I ask you to receive her in the Lord in a way worthy of his people and to give her any help she may need from you, for she has been the benefactor of many people, including me.

Greet Priscilla and Aquila, my co-workers in Christ Jesus. They risked their lives for me. Not only I but all the churches of the Gentiles are grateful to them.

Greet also the church that meets at their house.

Greet my dear friend Epenetus, who was the first convert to Christ in the province of Asia.

Greet Mary, who worked very hard for you.

Greet Andronicus and Junia, my fellow Jews who have been in prison with me. They are outstanding among the apostles, and they were in Christ before I was.

(Romans 16:1–7)

In the conclusion of his letter to the church in Rome, Paul listed off greetings to various church leaders, something he did often in all his letters. Yet this time it's significant because, in just the first seven verses of Romans 16, we see four women leaders listed: Phoebe, Prisca, Mary, and Junia. When we continue through the rest of the chapter these four women are joined by at least six others: Tryphena, Tryphosa, Persis (v. 12), Rufus's mother (v. 13), Julia, and Nereus's sister (v. 15). In addition, verse 14 also mentions "the other brothers and sisters with them," indicating that there were additional unnamed women Paul was acknowledging. At least a third of Paul's greetings to church leaders are for women, which might not seem significant to us today, but in the patriarchal culture in which Paul wrote, it is something to pay attention to.

When we revisit Prisca and Aquila in Romans 16, we once again see Prisca was apparently a prominent leader in the early church—so much so that Paul called her and Aquila "co-workers," a term that illustrates he viewed them as equal partners in the work of the church, especially when we consider that Paul himself never made it to Rome. When we look at the missionary work that Prisca, Aquila, and Paul did together in Ephesus, it is logical to conclude that Prisca and Aquila went back to their home in Rome and established a church (or multiple churches) there. It's likely they were awaiting Paul's arrival when Phoebe arrived in his stead (see Romans 16:1).

QUESTIONS FOR DISCUSSION OR REFLECTION

1. Do you find it believable that Prisca's name being listed before Aquila's is an indication of her more prominent leadership role? Why or why not? (Think about couples you know; whose name do you put first when you talk about them? Why?)

2. Do you think the pairing of Prisca and Aquila supports the previously introduced idea of two-by-two ministry pairs? Why or why not? How do you think Prisca and Aquila might have worked together in ministry?

PHOEBE AND JUNIA

Phoebe, the first woman listed in the Romans 16 text, was also a significant leader in the early church of Rome. However, unlike the other women listed, Phoebe was not greeted in the text; she was "commended," which indicates she probably didn't have a connection with the Roman church, so Paul was introducing her to them because she delivered the letter from Paul to the Roman church. There wasn't a mail system at that time for average people, so if you had a letter to send, you would have to find someone who would take it for you. In this case, Phoebe would have had to travel from her home Cenchreae, to Paul to get the letter, then on to Rome, a place she had likely never been before. She would then have to deliver the letter to the Roman Christians.

Remember that a large number of people were illiterate, so these letters would've been read to them. It is most likely that Phoebe read the letter herself, which means she would have had to understand it enough to be able to interpret it for the people listening and to answer any questions they had. Such an assignment would've required great trust on the part of Paul, and he chose to entrust this work to a woman.

Not only was Phoebe entrusted to deliver this important letter to the church, but she also was referred to as "a deacon of the church in Cenchreae." Recall that *diakanos* is a term that meant something akin to "minister." Phoebe, who appears in the text without mention of a male attachment, appears to have been a respected leader in her home church. Some believe she was widowed, but that text does not make that clear. What we do see is Paul describing her as a "benefactor of many" (v. 2), which means she had wealth, and probably property, as well as the financial means to fund a church and her own journey to Rome. Phoebe was clearly instrumental in the work of the church in Cenchreae, Rome, and beyond.

Another woman of significance in Romans 16 is Junia, listed in verse 7 alongside Andronicus. There's a great chance Andronicus was Junia's husband and that they were a ministry team, like Prisca and Aquila. Andronicus and Junia are noteworthy in the text for Paul's description of them as "outstanding among the apostles." Although early interpreters took the idea of Junia as a prominent apostle in stride, Paul's characterization of her caused an issue for some medieval church leaders, who saw it as problematic to refer to a woman as an apostle.

As a result, they began translating the name Junia as Junias, a more masculine-seeming name that is still found in some translations today. This reading implied that Paul was referring to two male disciples, and it gained serious traction when Martin Luther supported the name change in his own translation. However, scholars have found no evidence anywhere of the existence of any ancient use of the name Junias by men. Studying the earliest versions of Romans 16 available, scholars agree it is clear that the name is the feminine Junia.

Why should the term "apostle," when attributed to a woman, cause issues for church leaders? The term is used to refer to one who is sent out, and it is usually reserved for people who are commissioned by Jesus himself. Paul referred to himself as an apostle after his encounter with Jesus on the road to Damascus, viewing himself as one sent directly by Christ.

"Apostle" indicates one sent to declare the good news of Jesus, to preach and teach, and to lead the church. We have already seen in previous chapters that women were in fact sent out directly by Jesus to share the good news with others. Mary Magdalene was the most prominent figure—referred to as the apostle to the apostles—but there were others as well. It can even be argued that, since Paul makes note in verse 7 that Andronicus and Junia were Christians before he was, they could have been actual disciples of Jesus before his crucifixion, which would mean they were then part of the commissioning Jesus gave his disciples.

However, certain leaders in history who did not support the leadership of women decided that "apostle" should be a term reserved for leaders in the church, which led to Junia's erasure. It was easier for them to erase her than to admit that a woman could be sent as an apostle to declare the good news of Christ. Yet Romans 16 makes clear that Paul didn't have an issue referring to women as leaders, including Junia. She was sent out to share the gospel message, and it appears, through her work in the early church and beyond, that she was obedient.

QUESTIONS FOR DISCUSSION OR REFLECTION

1. Have you ever heard before that Phoebe was the messenger who brought the letter from Paul to the Roman church?

2. Why might Paul have trusted Phoebe with the letter? What kind of relationship and conversations would've had to happen between these two in order for Paul to be comfortable letting her not only carry and deliver the letter but also be the one who read it and answered questions about it?

3. How did you feel reading about how some Bible interpreters tried to erase a feminine Junia from Scripture?

PAUL AND WOMEN LEADERS

There are four additional women listed in Romans 16. Although they aren't given titles like "deacon" or "apostle" like Phoebe and Junia, they are described in various ways as hard workers (see vv. 6, 12). Mary, Tryphena, Tryphosa, and Persis are all listed with a description about their hard work accompanying their names. New Testament scholar Nijay Gupta tells us that "the Greek word Paul uses here, *kopiaō*, 'implies honorable toil for the sake of the gospel or the Christian community.' This verb carries the basic meaning of toil or difficult work, as in manual labor. But Paul had a tendency to use this as a semi-technical term for the hard work of ministry. In fact, he often used this for his apostolic work."

Without proper understanding, it would be easy to skip over these women in the text without much acknowledgment, but they were doing the work of ministry in the early church alongside the men. In fact, part of Paul's motivation in naming so many people in Romans 16 could have been to introduce them to one another. The church in Rome would've been more like a network of smaller gatherings in people's homes. They didn't have a central meeting place or building where everyone who was a Christian in Rome could go to gather or worship, so they did it in smaller groups. As the church grew, it would have become impossible for everyone to know everyone else. Paul's greetings in the conclusion of his letter could've been a way for the various and scattered members of the church to hear of the work and ministry of their fellow Roman Christians, and to see how the church was spreading in Rome.

Even though Paul named more men than women in his closing greetings and commendations, he reserved his highest descriptions of praise for the women. Gupta argues that this strategy was intentional: "Paul was explicitly commending women's ministry and leadership, perhaps even encouraging more Roman women to [lead]. If we aren't willing to go that far, we must at least acknowledge that Paul did not treat women differently than men when it came to church ministry and leadership." Indeed, Romans 16 shows us a model of church where women and men lead together to accomplish the hard work of the church.

Romans 16 is not the only place we can find evidence of women leading the early church. The church in Philippi also boasted a female leader, named Lydia, whose story can be found in Acts 16. Paul and Silas traveled on a missionary journey to Philippi, where they stayed for several days. While they were there, they went outside the city gate and down to the river, where they began to preach to the women gathered there:

> One of those listening was a woman from the city of Thyatira named Lydia, a dealer in purple cloth. She was a worshiper of God. The Lord opened her heart to respond to Paul's message. When she and the members of her household were baptized, she invited us to her home. "If you consider me a believer in the Lord," she said, "come and stay at my house." And she persuaded us.

(Acts 16:14–15)

Lydia is an example of an early church convert who extended hospitality to Paul and Silas. We know that she was a businesswoman, dealing in purple cloth, and that likely the home she invited Paul and Silas into was her own. She was the manager of the household.

Later, Paul and Silas got into some trouble with the townspeople in Philippi, and they were thrown into prison. When they were released, they went to Lydia's house again, "where they met with the brothers and sisters and encouraged them" (v. 40). This phrasing implies that a church was meeting in Lydia's home. Gupta tells us that this detail "is an important clue that Lydia had an immediate impact as a leader within the fledgling Christian community. She has passion, position, and means to host and lead the Christian community."

Another interesting place where we see evidence of women's leadership is the term *episkopoi* ("overseers") in Philippians 1:1, alongside *diakanoi* ("deacons"), when Paul brings greetings to the church there. This is important because the word *episkopa* is where the early church derived its word for "bishop." Gupta says we can't know for sure but that "it is more certain that two women explicitly mentioned in Paul's letter held one or the other of these ministry titles: Euodia and Syntyche." Euodia and Syntyche are named in Philippians 4:2–3. There seems to have been some sort of quarrel, though it is not explicitly explained, and Paul reminded them to be of one mind, an admonition that fits the overarching themes in Philippians, where Paul often pointed to unity in mission. Since both of these women were important enough to be named in the letter, and explicitly called "co-workers" with Paul, it is likely that one or both of them were being referred to as *episkopoi* or *diakanoi*.

The idea of women serving as bishops in the early church extends beyond the biblical text. Taylor and Ramelli share a known historical complaint from a religious leader in the fourth century:

> Around 371, Bishop Epiphanius of Salamis (c. 310–403) wrote the most detailed surviving description of women bishops. He complained, in the present tense, about a prophetic Christian movement with women bishops and women presbyters, and said: "They have women bishops, presbyters and the rest; they say that none of this makes any difference because 'in Christ Jesus, there is neither male nor female.'"

This bishop's complaint leads us to another New Testament text that is important in the conversation about women leaders:

"So in Christ Jesus you are all children of God through faith, for all of you who were baptized into Christ have clothed yourselves with Christ. There is neither Jew nor Gentile, neither slave nor free, nor is there male and female, for you are all one in Christ Jesus" (Galatians 3:26–28). Paul was emphasizing an egalitarian way of living. While the world around them was focused on status, ethnicity, or gender, citizens of the kingdom of God were now to be defined by their new life in Christ. This instruction represented a marked difference from the world around them. The culture around the early church was obsessed with status—how to have it, how to keep it, and how to get more of it. There were ranking systems in this patriarchal world, where men with money and influence were at the top and enslaved women languished at the bottom.

The early church communicated something completely different: in Christ, status wasn't important. They leaned into the teachings of Jesus that said the last would be first and the first last (Matthew 20:16). They embraced the idea that in order to be the greatest one must become a servant of all (Mark 9:35)—so much so that the word *diakanos*, which traditionally was known as "servant," eventually became synonymous with "church leader." Roles that were traditionally given to women—like the passing out of food—were switched up and given to men, as we read earlier; and roles that traditionally were given to men—like speaking publicly—were also available to women in the church.

When the church gathered together in those early days, they were to look at one another differently, as equals who were united in their love for Christ and for one another. They were united not because they came from the same status but because they were one in Christ. This unity enabled them to see *beyond* gender, to the power of the Holy Spirit given to all, allowing women to thrive in various leadership roles throughout the early church.

QUESTIONS FOR DISCUSSION OR REFLECTION

1. What sense do you get about Lydia? Why might it have been important for Acts to mention that she was a dealer in purple cloth?

2. Why might Paul and Silas have chosen to go straight to Lydia's house after being let out of prison?

3. What female leader in the early church stands out the most to you from this chapter? Why?

4. How has your view of the leadership of women changed after reading about the various roles of women in the early church?

5. Reread Galatians 3:26–28: "So in Christ Jesus you are all children of God through faith, for all of you who were baptized into Christ have clothed yourselves with Christ. There is neither Jew nor Gentile, neither slave nor free, nor is there male and female, for you are all one in Christ Jesus." How is your local church embodying this instruction from Paul?

6. How can we honor Paul's instruction about unity in Christ without erasing identities? Do you think he meant that we should pretend not to notice someone's skin color or gender at all?

SUGGESTIONS FOR FURTHER READING

Eldon Jay Epp, *Junia: The First Woman Apostle* (2005)

Paula Gooder, *Phoebe: A Story* (2018)

5

TRICKY BIBLE PASSAGES

←→

We have seen the evidence that Paul viewed women as equals, advocating for them, and celebrated them in various places of leadership throughout the church—which leads to the question, what about the places in Scripture where Paul seems to assert that women should not be in leadership in the church, or that they should be quiet?

Before we dive into these tricky passages, we need to remember that we look at the particulars of Scripture in light of the whole of Scripture. That is why this chapter comes so late in the book, after we have walked through so many other scriptural examples and read about so many women in various leadership roles among the people of God. Knowing the overall pattern for how women were viewed and treated across centuries becomes vital for when we begin to look at specific verses that have been historically used to bar women from leadership roles.

If only a few sections are preventing us from placing women in leadership, we must ask ourselves why these few verses hold so much weight over the rest of Scripture. Do we hold other areas of Scripture in the same high regard? Do we hold to the idea that women must cover their heads (1 Corinthians 11:5–6) with the same conviction that we bar women from leadership? If not, why? Could it be that something warrants further exploration and study?

In chapter 1, we explored 1 Corinthians 11 in depth with our conversation about what Paul might have meant when he used the Greek word *kephalē* ("head" or "source"). In light of what we've now discussed in the chapters about how Jesus treated women and how women participated in early church leadership, it might be worth the time to go back and reread that section in chapter 1. Reminding ourselves of the discussion about 1 Corinthians 11 will also help set the groundwork for the next difficult text, which is also found in 1 Corinthians.

1 CORINTHIANS 14

One of the most frequently used passages to prohibit women from serving as leaders in the church is 1 Corinthians 14:34–35: "Women should remain silent in the churches. They are not allowed to speak, but must be in submission, as the law says. If they want to inquire about something, they should ask their own husbands at home; for it is disgraceful for a woman to speak in the church." The challenge for us as modern readers of this passage is that it is difficult to fully understand what the social rules were around speech and silence in that culture.

New Testament scholar Susan Hylen helps paint a picture for us in her book *Women in the New Testament World* by using the following narrative:

103

Consider this example of modern rules for speech: American culture values freedom of expression, but if someone proclaims his or her political allegiances loudly in the middle of a movie, that individual will likely be thrown out of the theater. The cultural "rule" of free speech does not govern every situation. People within the culture do not usually experience silence in the movie theater as a contradiction of the rule of free speech. Culture provides the social understanding that shapes our speech and silence in particular situations. The same person may be silent in one place and speak forcefully in a different context, and in each case he or she may be operating well within the expected social norms.

This illustration from Dr. Hylen paints a picture that we can understand of a context in which we would be silent—not by force, not by command, but rather because of specific cultural expectations in that particular setting.

It is also helpful for us to understand that silence was a virtue in the culture and time period of the early church. It was synonymous with a life of self-control. Other places in the New Testament indicate the value of silence. James 1:19 says, "My dear brothers and sisters, take note of this: Everyone should be quick to listen, slow to speak and slow to become angry." Later in the same letter, James says,

> We all stumble in many ways. Anyone who is never at fault in what they say is perfect, able to keep their whole body in check. When we put bits into the mouths of horses to make them obey us, we can turn the whole animal. Or take ships as an example. Although they are so large and are driven by strong winds, they are steered by a very small rudder wherever the pilot wants to go. Likewise, the tongue is a

small part of the body, but it makes great boasts. Consider what a great forest is set on fire by a small spark. The tongue also is a fire, a world of evil among the parts of the body. It corrupts the whole body, sets the whole course of one's life on fire, and is itself set on fire by hell.

(James 3:2–6)

James helps us understand the value of silence as an important virtue for all Christians. Having the self-control to have a tame tongue was something to be revered, and would have been a sign of someone worth following, regardless of gender. Why, then, did Paul seem to direct his instruction for silence in 1 Corinthians 14 specifically toward women?

To answer this question, let's look at the larger textual context. This specific section of Scripture comes in the midst of broader instructions on worship in general. The church in Corinth, like all churches at the time, was brand new. They were trying to navigate what it meant to be a church, what worship looked like, and how to work together. In 1 Corinthians, Paul intended to create a guide for worship that wasn't chaotic and confusing. In a pagan city that was home to numerous pagan converts, it was important for Paul to disciple and guide his churches through understanding what it meant to engage in *Christian* worship as opposed to worship that some of them may have experienced in pagan contexts before converting to Christianity.

Throughout these instructions on worship (most significantly in chapters 10–14), women are not singled out as prohibited from full participation. In chapter 12, when Paul discusses spiritual gifts, he does not indicate that women might be excluded from certain giftings. Chapter 12 clearly states that the Holy Spirit gives gifts as the Holy Spirit determines. It doesn't seem to be dependent on gender but on the working of the Spirit. Chapter 11 specifically speaks to women prophesying and praying publicly, which is the opposite of silence. How can women prophesy and pray publicly if they are required to be silent? The question we need to ask in chapter 14 is, what does women being silent in this particular context have to do with worship that is ordered versus chaotic?

Some scholars have posited a theory that this particular instruction in chapter 14 wasn't written by Paul, since it looks so different from his other instructions and from the numerous places where he elevates and applauds the leadership of women. This theory suggests that these instructions were added later, to reflect a cultural imposition of the silence of women. The church was changing and growing, introducing hierarchy where there previously had been none, which is why it stands out so oddly among a variety of stories and passages where women speak, prophesy, pray, and lead.

New Testament scholar Lucy Peppiatt gives another theory that seems more plausible than that Paul simply didn't write that section of the letter. Peppiatt argues that, because Paul was raised in Greek culture and was a great orator, he likely spoke and argued using the predominant oration style of that time, which was a form of persuasive speech called rhetoric. Rhetoric, in order to refute the opposition, explains the opposing view in the way the opposing view would articulate itself. Rhetoric is a technique still commonly employed today in debates and persuasive prose.

The suggestion that Paul was using rhetoric is consistent with his teachings in other places where he quotes popular thought in order to argue against it. Thus, Peppiatt and other scholars believe Paul was doing the same thing in 1 Corinthians 14:34–35, verses that do read as an argument that would be given by the patriarchal culture at large, and the Corinthian church in particular. Peppiatt quotes another biblical scholar, Anthony Thiselton: "Many argue that vv. 34–35 represent a Corinthian slogan or piece of Corinthian theology which Paul quotes, only to reject it. Such a view is not farfetched, for Paul appears to do precisely this in 6:12; 7:1; 10:23; and perhaps elsewhere (e.g., 8:1–6)." Telling women to be silent in the churches, then, is not an admonition we are supposed to follow because it was not Paul commanding it but Paul quoting it in order to reject it.

Regardless of which theory about these particular verses is true, the text makes clear that the goal of Paul's correction was to facilitate orderly worship in a new church that struggled with what it meant to be a church. It is also clear that these are specific instructions given to a specific church. Although we can learn and appreciate a great deal from Paul's teachings in Scripture, we must be careful to understand them in the particular contexts they were written to address.

Fannie McDowell Hunter, a clergywoman from the early 1900s, boldly wrote in her book, *Women Preachers*, "Paul's prohibition—34th verse—was for that local church and was only temporary." McDowell Hunter went on to say, "If Paul meant literally for women not to prophesy or speak in the churches he was certainly self-contradictory. He not only permitted but encouraged the public ministry of women as he gives them instructions on how they are to pray and prophesy (1 Cor. 11:5, 6)." Jaime Clark-Soles emphasizes the same when she says, "It would be awfully difficult to simultaneously pray and prophesy in church (as do the women in 1 Cor. 11) while also 'shutting up.'"

QUESTIONS FOR DISCUSSION OR REFLECTION

1. What do you think about the word "silence" as being connected with self-control?

2. Which theory about 1 Corinthians 14 do you think sounds the most plausible?
   - That Paul intended for women to be silent in churches, contradicting things he wrote previously?

   - That someone other than Paul retroactively inserted verses 34 and 35 to reflect changing culture in the church?

   - That Paul was quoting a popular opposing argument from his own time period in order to refute it?

3. Look up and read 1 Corinthians 14:34–40. If Paul intended to use rhetoric in verses 34 and 35 in order to reject an opposing viewpoint, how do verses 36–40 reject it?

4. What are your thoughts on Susan Hylen's movie theater analogy and the discussion about appropriate times and places for certain behaviors?

1 TIMOTHY 2

We closed the previous section with Jaime Clark-Soles's assertion, "It would be awfully difficult to simultaneously pray and prophesy in church (as do the women in 1 Cor. 11) while also 'shutting up.'" Clark-Soles isn't only referencing the admonition to be silent in 1 Corinthians, though. She is also talking about 1 Timothy 2:8–15:

Therefore I want the men everywhere to pray, lifting up holy hands without anger or disputing. I also want the women to dress modestly, with decency and propriety, adorning themselves, not with elaborate hairstyles or gold or pearls or expensive clothes, but with good deeds, appropriate for women who profess to worship God.

A woman should learn in quietness and full submission. I do not permit a woman to teach or to assume authority over a man; she must be quiet. For Adam was formed first, then Eve. And Adam was not the one deceived; it was the woman who was deceived and became a sinner. But women will be saved through childbearing—if they continue in faith, love and holiness with propriety.

There is a lot to unpack in these few verses, and it is important for us to work through all of it to get a better picture of what was going on in this church in Ephesus, and what 1 Timothy is saying both in the fuller textual context and in the cultural and historical contexts.

First, "modesty" is a word that is deeply connected to culture, so when we read it, we automatically bring our own definition to the table. We might picture an ankle-length skirt or a turtleneck sweater. It may conjure up for us hurtful memories of school dress codes. Whatever specific image we may get individually, twenty-first-century readers as a whole almost always think of clothing in connection to the word "modesty"—in particular, clothing that covers up certain body parts. In the world of 1 Timothy, modesty means something more than just how someone dresses. It is connected with personal conduct and character. In fact, the Greek word for modesty is closely connected with the word for self-control.

Additionally, Lucy Peppiatt reminds us that there is an implicit understanding that the letter is addressing women who were previously part of the Artemis cult, so now they are being instructed not to dress in the same ways they would have been expected to dress in order to serve Artemis. Sometimes verse 9 is translated as "braids" instead of "elaborate hairstyles," which Peppiatt says seems to refer to the hairstyles and clothing that "wealthy priestesses wore in cultic activities. No wonder there was a need to shed (literally) this apparel and replace it with modest clothing, no longer associating with pagan worship."

The women who belonged to the cult of Artemis were generally wealthy women. Elaborate hairstyles would have taken time—and often servants or slaves—to achieve. The Artemis cult was based on status and wealth, and the flaunting of both. Telling new converts to have self-control and humility in the way they dress was a way of telling them that the kingdom of God works differently. In the kingdom of God, everyone is welcome to participate regardless of status or financial standing—in fact, the least are the greatest in God's kingdom. This instruction to dress with humility is less about covering up certain body parts in the way that we imagine modest and humble dress today, and more about understanding and participating fully in the kingdom of God, whose ways counter the kingdoms and cults of the world. The women involved with the cult of Artemis were often known for doing good deeds. Their deeds and donations were very public, in contrast to the instruction of 1 Timothy, where the text seems to indicate that good deeds are to be done for God alone.

Verse 11 is the most difficult part of this passage: "A woman should learn in quietness and full submission." When taken away from the context of the previous verses and the cultural context we have just been discussing, it is easy to see why this verse by itself has been used to keep women out of leadership. However, when set in its proper context, it becomes clearer that the writer is continuing the instructions on exhibiting self-control and the importance of learning. The phrase "should learn" is the active verb in this text. That is the part of the verse that is emphasized. Women *should learn.*

This imperative is important in a culture where we assume that only men were formally educated. Women are being commanded here to learn about Scripture, to be students. The appropriate posture for a student is self-control, exhibited by quietness and submission as they learn what is being taught. This is less a prohibition toward women, then, and more an illustration of how students are to learn, coupled with a command that women are to be included *among* students, not separated out—especially because many of them are coming from the Artemis cult. These women need to take time to be quiet and learn what it means to be a follower of Christ. They must listen and be discipled first, before taking on leadership in this church. Peppiatt quotes Bible scholar Ben Witherington, who says, "Paul was facing the reality of high-status women who expect to play a religious role in the Christian meetings but have not yet been fully or properly instructed in the apostolic teaching." Because these women came from places of influence and status, they joined the church with the same posture, automatically expecting to be granted leadership and assuming leadership roles without actually knowing yet what they are talking about.

The Greek word translated as "authority" in verse 12 (*authentein*) has become of particular interest to scholars because this verse is the only place it ever appears in the whole Bible (yet another reason to view this section as a particular passage for a particular people at a particular time). There are a few different translation options for *authentain*, including "exercise authority" or "domineer," or it could be connected to the idea of the person as "author" or "originator." It seems most likely that the word represents some combination of these options. Thus, Peppiatt says,

> the prohibition on teaching is against the teaching of heresy linked to the Artemis/Isis cult. If women . . . are joining the church, it is easily imaginable how they end up assuming authority, control, and might have taken to teaching others without seeing the need to receive instruction. . . . Paul's use of the word *authentein* would have carried with it the connotations that woman must cease propagating heresy that promoted the woman as the usurper of authority from man, the woman as the originator of man, and that man was the one deceived in the creation account. These verses are aimed at the confident female teachers of a particular Greek/Egyptian heresy that warrants this response.

Verses 12–14, then, do not represent a commandment for all women everywhere in all times, but only in this particular place and context.

Knowing this context helps us as we consider how we build up leaders in churches today. Although most local churches are not operating at the center of a competing religious cult like the cult of Artemis in Ephesus, there are very strong cultural and religious allegiances in our world, and those allegiances are hard to break when someone becomes a Christian. It is important for all of us to become learners—and to encourage others to learn—before assuming leadership roles, lest we teach things that counter the gospel message of Jesus. It could even be argued that a patriarchal hierarchy is one of the practices the church has adopted from the world instead of from God. It would be good for all of us—men and women—to give attention to learning well before we presume to teach.

Finally, we come to the perplexing verse 15: "But women will be saved through childbearing. . . ." This verse stands out as odd for many reasons. First, it contradicts Paul's other statements about how unmarried men and women can be wholly "concerned about the Lord's affairs," without the worldly encumbrances that spouses bring (see 1 Corinthians 7). If Paul believed that women were saved through childbirth, then why would he advocate for the unmarried men and women to stay single? The idea of women being saved through childbirth, on its face, is starkly opposed to Paul's strong belief of salvation through faith. Childbirth does not save women; rather, the grace of Jesus through faith does. So why mention childbirth at all?

Scholar Sandra Glahn has studied and written in depth about the Artemis cult in Ephesus, and Peppiatt references Glahn's scholarship and quotes her explanation that, according to the Ephesian myth, Artemis witnessed the painful birth of her brother Apollo and, as a result, determined never to give birth herself. She asked her father, Zeus, to make her immune to the arrows of Aphrodite (the goddess of love), and Zeus granted her request. Artemis then became associated with virginity and with midwifery, becoming a "'powerful, volatile sovereign who determines who will live or die.' Artemis was believed either to be able to deliver a mother and child safely through childbirth or alternatively to dispatch the mother in labor as a form of mercy killing should the labor be too long and too torturous. Thus the name of Artemis was associated with one who had the power to deliver and, crucially, became associated with the term 'savior.'"

Women in the New Testament world were terrified of childbirth because they felt they were under the watchful eye of Artemis, who alone could save or destroy them. When we look at the full context of 1 Timothy 2, it becomes clear that Paul is reframing the idea of childbirth. Women don't have to fear Artemis because they are following the true Savior, and they will be saved. The word "saved" here is not about salvation in the Christian sense but about deliverance from constant fear. Peppiatt tells us that Glahn concludes, "Paul takes a familiar phrase and reframes it for his audience. Being saved by childbearing is not within Artemis's purview, as they had been taught, but God's."

Set in its proper context, we can clearly see that these verses in 1 Timothy 2 do not communicate subordination and oppression for women but inclusion, freedom, and hope.

QUESTIONS FOR DISCUSSION OR REFLECTION

1. How does this reframing of a passage that seems quite harsh and misogynistic on its surface help you understand its positive message for women?

2. Why do you think Paul specifies women in this passage instead of saying that all new converts should observe silently and take on the posture of students before attempting to assume leadership roles?

3. If 1 Timothy 2:8–15 is a passage written for a particular people belonging to a particular culture at a particular time in history, what significance should these verses hold for us today?

1 TIMOTHY 3

Our final tricky passage is 1 Timothy 3:1–13:

Here is a trustworthy saying: Whoever aspires to be an overseer desires a noble task. Now the overseer is to be above reproach, faithful to his wife, temperate, self-controlled, respectable, hospitable, able to teach, not given to drunkenness, not violent but gentle, not quarrelsome, not a lover of money. He must manage his own family well and see that his children obey him, and he must do so in a manner worthy of full respect. (If anyone does not know how to manage his own family, how can he take care of God's church?) He must not be a recent convert, or he may become conceited and fall under the same judgment as the devil. He must also have a good reputation with outsiders, so that he will not fall into disgrace and into the devil's trap.

In the same way, deacons are to be worthy of respect, sincere, not indulging in much wine, and not pursuing dishonest gain. They must keep hold of the deep truths of the faith with a clear conscience. They must first be tested; and then if there is nothing against them, let them serve as deacons.

In the same way, the women are to be worthy of respect, not malicious talkers but temperate and trustworthy in everything.

A deacon must be faithful to his wife and must manage his children and his household well. Those who have served well gain an excellent standing and great assurance in their faith in Christ Jesus.

One of the biggest issues in this text is the translation. We come to this text, as we have so many others, with our own biases and presuppositions. In this text, the NIV translates the pronouns as "he" in places where the Greek text doesn't do that. The Greek pronouns used are plural, which means they could pertain to women *or* men, and many scholars agree that this text addresses both men and women. This passage is about virtues and qualities that apply to anyone in a leadership position regardless of gender. In fact, verse 11 directly names women, and verse 12—which, in Greek, uses plural nouns and pronouns rather than singular, as the English NIV does—goes on to specifically call them deacons. Since Paul repeatedly names female deacons throughout his letters, a reference to women as deacons here would not be a surprise.

The challenge that still remains is the phrase "faithful to his wife" that appears in verses 2 and 12. The actual translation is "one woman man." In fact, Lucy Peppiatt quotes scholar William Witt on the matter: "With the single exception of the three-word expression 'one woman man' . . . nothing in the passage would indicate that the person being discussed for the office of overseer/bishop would be either a man or a woman." Yet these verses have been used to bar women from serving in the church, since they cannot be a "one woman man." Again we run up against the issue of language. Some scholars claim that Paul is first addressing male deacons and then female deacons in the text. Peppiatt shares Ben Witherington's opinion, which says the entire passage rests on the word "must" in verse 2 and that each subsequent role must also exhibit the characteristics of the other church role. Therefore, when we arrive at verse 11, where it specifically speaks to women, their role also includes the other qualities.

The phrase "one woman man" is also used when explaining self-control. The idea is that this is a person who exhibits self-control. Given that the rest of the text could be applied to men or women, it is not farfetched to believe that the phrase "one woman man" is less about a man being the only person able to hold leadership and more about a colloquial expression about self-control. Regardless of what "one woman man" means, the textual context shows us that women are included in leadership in this passage.

QUESTIONS FOR DISCUSSION OR REFLECTION

1. Why do you think the NIV decided to translate nouns and pronouns that are plural in the Greek, into the singular in this passage?

2. Some say that masculine pronouns and other masculine nouns (like "mankind") are meant to represent all humans, regardless of gender. How helpful is this explanation? How do you think people would feel if the chosen nouns and pronouns meant to represent everybody were feminine instead of masculine?

3. Read aloud a different translation of 1 Timothy 3:1–12. Choose a version that uses plural nouns and pronouns (such as the NRSVUE). How do you receive the passage differently, and how does that difference make you feel about trusting just one English translation?

SCRIPTURE AS A WHOLE

These few passages from 1 Corinthians and 1 Timothy are often the ones people reference when trying to deny women leadership in the church. Why do we focus on these particular verses, removed from their surrounding context, instead of looking at the totality of Scripture? When else do we reinterpret or disregard the whole of Scripture in favor of a few specific verses? We have walked together through the Old Testament's example of feminine leadership, through the life of Jesus as he relates to women in the New Testament, and we've even dived into the early church. We have seen women in leadership positions throughout Scripture from beginning to end—yet the few verses in these select passages have prevented so many women from stepping into and fulfilling the leadership roles to which God has called them.

Understanding the cultural context for these passages not only opens these women up to the freedom available to them in Christ, but it also expands for us a beautiful image of what the church has been and can be in the world—because, at the heart of it all, we see a church that is growing in hard places. We are seeing leaders raised up in places where paganism had a strong hold. We see stories of lives transformed because of the work of the Holy Spirit and the faithfulness of Jesus's followers.

When we are all free to serve Jesus through the power of the Holy Spirit, the world is changed, and lives are transformed. That was true in the early church, and it has continued to be true throughout time.

QUESTIONS FOR DISCUSSION OR REFLECTION

1. Why do you think we focus on these particular scriptures when talking about women in ministry, instead of looking at all of the stories of women as leaders in the Bible?

2. What did you learn about the cult of Artemis?

3. When we consider the added context about the cult of Artemis and why Paul had to address those women specifically, what does it teach us about how we should prepare and train leaders in our current context?

4. What stood out to you the most in this chapter as something you need to remember? Why does that particular point stand out to you?

SUGGESTIONS FOR FURTHER READING

Sandra L. Glahn, *Nobody's Mother: Artemis of the Ephesians in Antiquity and the New Testament* (2023)

Susan Hylen, *Women in the New Testament World* (2019)

6
WESLEYAN-HOLINESS WOMEN LEADERS
←→

In the previous pages we have studied a "mighty throng" of women proclaiming the word of the Lord, like Psalm 68:11 declares. We have wrestled with what it means that women are created in the image of God and what it means that daughters will prophesy. There have been roadblocks, hurdles, and discouragement for women throughout history who have been called to preach, teach, and take on a variety of leadership roles inside the church. Yet, despite these hurdles, God has continued to call women, and women have faithfully responded.

In the early church, the stories of female martyrs became a profound source of hope and evangelism in the world. Lynn Cohick and Amy Brown Hughes tell us in their book *Christian Women in the Patristic World*, "It is possible that as many women were martyred as men. . . . The martyr's death was not a respecter of gender." These martyr deaths of early women are an important form of church leadership because the martyrs defied the expectations placed on women to be committed solely to their families. Cohick and Hughes say, "Through the martyrs' actions and words, the early church forged a new model of community and familial responsibilities, which rightly shocked the ancient world." While we could, probably rightfully, critique the way of the martyr, we cannot deny the incredible impact martyrs had on the church and the ways they communicated their hope in the resurrection, even unto death. Not only that, but for female martyrs in particular, we are reminded by Cohick and Hughes that "the gospel was so strong, the church could argue that by its power even a weak [woman] was made stronger than the strongest warrior."

The early church had women like Perpetua and Felicitas, both mothers who died in the arena rather than give allegiance to pagan gods. Perpetua's father begged her to forsake Christ and live, and she refused in an incredible boldness during an era of extreme patriarchy, where the father was head over everything. Felicitas gave birth in prison before being sent to die a brutal death. Both women trusted in the hope of Jesus and in the church to care for their children. Stories like these were told regularly in the early church, giving hope to people who were struggling and suffering.

Women continued to serve the church in profound ways, and in the fourth century a woman named Egeria wrote a book called *Travels of Egeria*, or *The Itinerary of Egeria*. It was a detailed account of her pilgrimage to and through the Holy Land. As Egeria traveled, she wrote of her experiences, including hearing women singing in congregations and churches—significant because some in the early church contested not only the *leadership* of women but also the *singing* of women because of scriptures pertaining to the silence of women. However, Egeria notes that "the churches and martyr shrines . . . were alive with worship, including women's voices singing psalms." Egeria's journey and writing created a new genre of literature that deeply influenced the church for generations. Cohick and Hughes point out that Egeria's writing also "reminds us that women's voices were heard in church singing and reading Scripture at holy sites, women's bodies were present at shrines and religious processions, and women engaged with men in theological discussions. Women were part of the making of the early church."

The Holy Spirit continued to move in the lives of women through the centuries. We have writings about Macrina, written by her brother, the bishop Gregory of Nyssa, who gives Macrina a lot of credit for being his theological teacher and guide.

Monica, the mother of Augustine, is not only the one who weeps over Augustine's salvation but also "is the expert on all of the really important stuff. . . . Augustine as the facilitator often defers to her and gives her the last word on many topics." It's safe to say Augustine would not have become a prominent church father without Monica.

In the fifth century there were women leaders in and around Rome. There is evidence of women bishops in art and literature around the city. In the Chapel of San Venantius there is an image of Mary the mother of Jesus wearing the episcopal pallium, an article of clothing portraying her as an archbishop. According to Taylor and Ramelli, the title of *episcopa* ("bishop") was used for women in Rome until at least "as late as Pope Paschal 1 (ruled 817–24), because Paschal twice commemorated his mother, Theodora, as *episcopa*." There is even a mosaic of Theodora in the

Basilica of Santa Prassede that clearly has the title *EPISCOPA* over her head and name.

In the medieval era, the first book written in the English language by a woman was *Revelations of Divine Love*, by Julian of Norwich, an anchoress who devoted her life to the church in profound ways. (An anchoress was someone who lived their life in a closed-off room of the church.) People traveled from afar to receive advice and counsel from Julian, and her words continue to inspire people today. We also still read words from Catherine of Siena, who is considered a doctor of the church, and whose political peacemaking and deep devotion to God and love for the church changed the entire landscape of the Western church.

It is difficult to find a moment in church history that hasn't been impacted by the leadership of women who were called by God to do important and diverse work. Women were teachers, writers, preachers, bishops, singers, scholars, theologians, and mystics. Although we have not devoted much time to so many years of history, it is important to declare and acknowledge that women were there, and they were leading. There has never been a time when the Holy Spirit wasn't calling women.

It is with all of this history of the church in mind that we arrive at the women who laid the foundation for the Wesley-an-Holiness movement. The Wesleyan-Holiness movement is not unique for having the sudden notion that women should be involved. Instead, Wesleyan-Holiness people knew that women had always been called by God in one way or another and that women had found creative ways to serve Christ boldly even with prohibitions and challenges in their path.

Susie Stanley's *Holy Boldness* starts with Madame Jeane Marie Bouvier de la Mothe Guyon as one who laid the foundation for the Wesleyan movement. Madame Guyon was a French Roman Catholic who was born in 1648 and died in 1717. Her writings on Christian perfection influenced John Wesley as he began to form his thoughts about sanctification and holiness. According to Stanley, Wesley even said, "Upon the whole, we may search many centuries before we find another woman who was such a pattern of true holiness."

Guyon had a clear call of God in her life. She gave spiritual counsel to many, including bishops, and she became widely sought after by people seeking what it meant to be holy. Her continued work gathered a significant following, which in turn led to significant persecution. Her own family and friends turned against her, and she was accused and imprisoned on more than one occasion for heresy. Yet, despite hardship, Guyon followed her call by writing theology and caring for others. Stanley says about her:

She actively responded to what she understood to be God's will: that she expand her ministry through spiritual counseling and writing. She sought to meet the needs of the poor. When persecuted, she did not passively accept her plight. Instead, she fought back, defending herself against false accusations and malicious rumors. Rather than quietly accepting the judgment of her opponents, she prepared a written justification of her theology. In this way, she also served as a prototype for her Wesleyan-Holiness daughters.

The Methodist movement was born, and with it were women who were called to leadership in the church. Mary Bosanquet Fletcher and Hester Ann Roe Rogers were friends and co-laborers of John Wesley. In fact, Stanley says that "historian Earl Kent Brown recovered information about forty-five Methodist women who were class and/or band meeting leaders and twenty-seven women preachers who were contemporaries of John Wesley." Stanley also tells us that Fletcher and Rogers "engaged in ministries normally considered outside the realm of women's appropriate behavior, and their lives and their writings justified their public activities." Although we often focus on the men who championed the Methodist movement, it's important to note that Methodists—along with other groups, like Quakers—were religious dissenters toward the Church of England, and one of the characteristics of these dissenting groups was that they supported women preachers. Quakers held the largest number of women preachers at the time, but Methodist women joined them in a public way in England in the 1700s.

Fletcher started an orphanage, where she preached regularly after receiving a call to preach from God in a dream. She then began to have more preaching engagements that led to her traveling, and it is noted that at one point she preached to a group of two or three thousand, even while facing opposition from those who thought she shouldn't be preaching. Despite the opposition, she continued on in the work she was called to, claiming that she did only "but what Mr. Wesley approves."

As Wesleyan-Holiness movements spread to the United States, women received calls to preach there as well. Antoinette Brown became the first ordained woman in the United States after her family was impacted by the revival preacher Charles Finney. Brown received a call to preach and sought theological education at Oberlin College, which was met with great opposition. According to Rebecca Laird in her book about ordained women, "Antoinette and another female student, Lettice Smith, were allowed to sit in on courses and do the academic work, but 'were excused' from participation in discussion, debates, or rhetorical exhibitions. They learned to write; men learned to write *and* to speak. . . . Public speaking was considered unseemly for proper young ladies." Despite the opposition, Blackwell was invited to pastor a church in South Butler, New York in 1853. On September 15, 1853, she was ordained by Rev. Luther Lee, who, according to Laird, preached:

> I do not believe that any special or specific form of ordination is necessary to constitute a gospel minister. We are not here to make a minister. It is not ours to confer on this our sister a right to preach the gospel. If she has not that right already, we have no power to communicate it to her. Nor have we met to qualify her for the work of the ministry. If God and mental and moral culture have not already qualified her, we cannot, by anything we may do by way of ordaining or setting her apart. . . . All we are here to do, and all we expect to do, is, in due form, and by a solemn and impressive service, to subscribe our testimony to the fact that in our belief, our sister in Christ, Antoinette L. Brown, is one of the ministers of the New Covenant, authorized, qualified, and called of God to preach the gospel of his Son Jesus Christ.

At the same time as the preaching of Antoinette Brown, Phoebe Palmer began a ministry that popularized the Wesleyan-Holiness movement in the United States. Palmer was never ordained. In fact, she thought ordained clergy were unnecessary, but she preached at revivals throughout the U.S. She was also a writer, a lay theologian, and an advocate of women's empowerment by the Holy Spirit. Palmer preached to tens of thousands worldwide and laid a foundation for the Wesleyan-Holiness women who came after her.

Although white women in the U.S. faced significant gender-related challenges in following their divine call to preach, teach, and serve in ministry leadership roles, Black women who were called and empowered by the Holy Spirit had to confront both sexism *and* racism in the church. Jarena Lee was the first woman preacher in the African Methodist Episcopal Church, and Amanda Smith, Zilpha Elaw, and Julia Foote were Black women preachers early in the Wesleyan-Holiness movement. These sanctified women found empowerment to preach the Word in a challenging world through the power of the Holy Spirit. According to Susie Stanley, Lee even used the term "holy energy" when speaking about the empowerment women experienced as they participated in public ministry.

In 1905, Fannie McDowell Hunter wrote a small book called *Women Preachers,* where she takes readers on a journey through Scripture, calling the church to realize that women belong in leadership roles. Toward the end of the book she shares several autobiographies of women preachers from the time, beginning with her own. Hunter shares about how she struggled to believe she was a Christian at all, and prayed deeply and fervently that she would receive an assurance of her faith. She said she had this profound experience of peace come upon her and that, "with this sweet experience came a love for perishing souls. They were constantly before me, helpless, sunken deeply in sin and vice. Their woes appealed to my heart. . . . Not only that, but I heard the sweet, confiding voice of the resurrected Christ to women saying 'go tell.'" So go Fannie did, becoming an evangelist who sang and preached, following the call of Christ and leading many to Christ. *Women Preachers* shares the stories of numerous other women who followed the call of God during and prior to Hunter's lifetime, encouraging and inspiring readers to recognize that the Holy Spirit was still calling women to the work of the ministry.

There are too many women for me to write about in the early Wesleyan-Holiness years. They were evangelists who preached at camp meetings, served in prison ministries, railroad ministries, and urban ministries, created homes for prostitutes, and ministered to the disenfranchised of their time. They fought for rights for women, and some stood against racism. Women were called by God in numerous places and spaces, and they continued to answer the call in the years ahead. Evangeline Booth—daughter of Catherine and William Booth, who founded the Salvation Army—was actively involved in leadership, notably sending 250 volunteers to care for soldiers during World War I. In 1935 Evangeline was elected general of the Salvation Army by the high council and led the entire international organization.

As women continued to answer God's call to ministry, the 1920s, '30s, and '40s brought increasing opposition to women's participation and leadership in ministry. Denominations like the Church of the Nazarene never changed their position on ordaining women, but society had changed, making it increasingly more difficult for women to be offered the leadership mantle. Rebecca Laird quoted an anonymous woman pastor from that time who said, "At preachers' meetings, assemblies, etc., when the men gather together in informal groups and discussions, and their wives congregate by themselves, I find I am 'neither beast, fowl, nor good red herring.' Though oftentimes as an afterthought I am invited into some group (usually of the wives) as though they felt, 'Poor dear, what *shall* we do with '*her*?'"

Laird explains that, by this time, "an ambivalence toward women in the ordained ministry had taken over. The church officially said yes to women seeking ordination while the middle-class culture that dominated the pews said no. . . . The Spirit that blew at Pentecost still was calling God's daughters to prophesy, but the church of the mid-twentieth century encouraged women to put family first and then declared the way to do so was to stay at home." Although women have always been called to do the work of ministry, their ability to respond to that call matters and can have a tremendous impact. In the case of these three early decades in the twentieth century, it was challenging to find women preachers and leaders during that time because the church chose to allow worldly culture to influence it in dramatic and unfortunate ways.

Even so, there women continued to answer God's call. Mildred Bangs Wynkoop was born in 1905 and went on to gain a rich theological education from Northwest Nazarene College, Pasadena College, Western Evangelical Seminary, and the University of Oregon, eventually attaining a doctorate of theology from Northern Baptist Theological Seminary. Wynkoop spent twenty years pastoring with her husband. She also spent time as an evangelist, then went on to teach at Western Evangelical Seminary. Following her time at Western, she taught in Japan from 1961 until 1966, where she was the founding president of Japan Theological Seminary. She then came back to the United States, where she taught theology and was the director of missions at Trevecca Nazarene College, followed by three years as the theologian-in-residence at Nazarene Theological Seminary. Her book

A *Theology of Love* is considered a groundbreaking and important work on holiness for an entire generation and beyond of Wesleyan-Holiness theologians and pastors. She continues to impact the church to this day, and will far into the future.

As time went on, and women began studying the early Wesleyan-Holiness movement, more and more women responded to the call, of whom Susie Stanley was one. Stanley's call to the ministry came in conjunction with her call to do work to elevate the voices of women. In an interview I held with Stanley several months before her death in 2022, she told me:

> In 1975 I received my call at an evangelical women's caucus. I was in a workshop on nineteenth-century women who had been called to ministry, but none of their denominations would ordain them. I thought, *Whoa, my church ordains women! What am I doing sitting here?* So that was my call to ministry. The question that remained for me was, if those women couldn't be ordained in the nineteenth century, what do we need to do today to have women ordained who are called? It was clear that my call was to minister to women who were called to minister.

Stanley went on to be ordained in 1983 in the Church of God (Anderson) and received her PhD from Iliff School of Theology in order to fulfill her call. Stanley went on to teach at Western Seminary and Messiah College, and published her book, *Holy Boldness*, about women preachers from the early days of the movement.

In 1987, while flying home from an academic conference, Stanley had the idea that it would be great to get all of the women clergy from various Wesleyan-Holiness denominations together in one place. The pooling of resources would enable there to be a larger group of women who could achieve more. The group that Susie dreamed of gathered together for the first time in April 1994 in Glorietta, New Mexico. About four hundred women gathered. In the *Christianity Today* article called "The Stained-Glass Ceiling" that Timothy Morgan wrote about the event, Wilbur Brannon (a pastoral ministries director in the Church of the Nazarene) was quoted as saying, "I'm afraid [there] has been an influence from those sectors of conservative Christianity which disallow the use of women. We need to reaffirm the specific values that are inherent in the Wesleyan tradition and in our Holiness movement." The Wesleyan-Holiness Women Clergy Conference has continued to meet faithfully since 1994 because of the vision of Susie Stanley and the original four hundred women who responded to the call.

In the vein of a Pauline epistle, it is my desire to tell you the story of every woman clergy in this great movement, but there isn't time to highlight everyone, so of whom shall I tell you?

Linda Adams was the first female bishop elected in the Free Methodist Church in 2019, paving the way for other women leaders throughout the denomination, including Kaye Kolde, who became the second woman elected as bishop in 2023. Bishop Adams and Bishop Kolde both responded to the call of the Spirit in a unique way after years of faithful service as pastors in their local churches.

Jo Anne Lyons was elected the first female general superintendent of the Wesleyan Church in 2008. She was ordained in 1998, the same year she founded World Hope International, and she also served as a preacher, teacher, and leader in numerous capacities.

Nina Gunter was ordained as an elder in the Church of the Nazarene in 1960 and, after years of faithful service, was elected the first female general superintendent in the Church of the Nazarene in 2005.

Carla Sunberg became the first woman president of Nazarene Theological Seminary in 2014 and the second female general superintendent in the Church of the Nazarene in 2017.

These leaders are stained-glass-ceiling breakers, and there remain so many *more* women answering the call to ministry throughout the world. I know many stories, and can list many names, but I don't know any story better than my own. While I may not be a stained-glass-ceiling breaker, let me offer my own story as a testimony that the Spirit of God still calls women today.

I was the first woman I ever heard preach. I was sixteen years old, and I called it "sharing." The urge started like a fire in my belly—a small spark at first that was easy to ignore, only to continue to be flamed until I felt I would burst. The desire became so hard to ignore that I emailed my church board and asked if I could share on a Sunday. To my surprise, they agreed. It's weird to look back on now. I'm sure my words were shaky and that my exegesis left something to be desired, but it was the beginning of a journey that continues today. I stepped behind a pulpit, not even knowing if that was a place I was allowed to be—which says something of the strong call of the Holy Spirit and the tenacity of sixteen-year-old girls.

I didn't attend a big church in a big city. I attended a little Nazarene church in a little town that most people have never heard of. My pastor is probably never going to be invited onstage at a General Assembly or applauded in a bestselling book, but if it weren't for that little local congregation and that pastor's confidence in God's call on my life (a call I pushed against, and he pushed back—every time), I wouldn't be here. When I was a senior in high school and freshman in college, this pastor put me on the preaching schedule nearly once a month on Sunday nights—a bold risk for a pastor to take on behalf of any gender at that age.

The only reason I even began to call it preaching was that my pastor told me outright, "Stop calling it 'speaking' and 'sharing.' Call it preaching because that's what it is." If it weren't for that moment, I don't know if I ever could have envisioned myself as a *preacher*. You can't call yourself a pastor or preacher if you are never told that you can preach; you simply become a teacher or a motivational speaker. I began calling myself a preacher while still being the only woman I had ever heard preach. I had no idea what it looked like or what it would be like, but I had people in my corner telling me it was possible who, beyond all odds, kept putting me behind the pulpit and listening to what I had to say.

I was well into college before I heard another woman who wasn't me preach for the first time—a reality I look back on with little bit of sadness and loneliness. I walked so very much alone in those early years, but the rebel in me also walked a little defiantly, that no one would take away what I felt God had placed within me. If it weren't for the defiant, small congregation and the small-church pastor telling me I could do it, I don't know if I would have pushed ahead as much as I did. However, what I heard when I heard myself preach, and still hear today, is that God uses ordinary, weird, broken, flawed people to do great things for the kingdom of God. I was a nobody—from a little town and a little church, a girl who loved books more than movies and running barefoot through the woods—and God still used me. God still called me, where I was, in spite of everything that was seemingly stacked against me.

It's no secret that sometimes it takes knowing the right people to get ahead (sadly, even in the church world). It takes a certain last name, or a relationship with someone who has a certain last name, or a connection with someone else who has a relationship with someone who has a certain last name. I had none of those. All I had was this ever-growing fire in my belly that would only subside if I preached. If God can call and use a young female preacher who had never heard a woman preach before—a nobody from a nothing town—what can God do in the lives of those young women who never have to be *told* to call it preaching because they already know that women can preach because they've already seen it? I can only imagine great things.

Decades have passed since the first time I preached behind a pulpit. Now I step behind a pulpit nearly every week in my little urban church in a town that, although bigger than my hometown, doesn't rank very high in levels of significance. I have had the privilege to learn from women professors and preachers in a seminary that encourages and supports women in leadership in all levels of the church. I have gotten to serve on the Nazarene Women Clergy council, advocate for women clergy across North America and around the world, and serve on the planning committee for the Wesleyan-Holiness Women Clergy Conference. What I have discovered is that answering the call is not easy— there have certainly been obstacles and challenges—but serving Jesus faithfully has always been worth it.

There are thousands of stories like mine. The details are different and the roles varied, yet girls and women around the world are sensing that fire in their bellies that won't subside. They aren't all serving in the highest levels of leadership—in fact, most of them aren't. Yet each and every day they wake up seeking to follow Jesus to the best of their ability.

They are doing rural ministry, often in small churches and small communities that most of us have never heard of.

They are ministering to children and teenagers, reminding us that people of all ages are welcomed into the kingdom of God and that Jesus called the children to come to him.

They are ministering to people on the margins who are often overlooked. Whether it is ministry in the disabled community, to living in poverty, or in immigrant communities, these ministers are exceptionally gifted at making the table of Christ inclusive for all.

They are ministering to people through spiritual direction and counseling.

They are ministering to people in big cities, navigating the complexities of urban life.

They are ministering to people through education—writing, teaching, and training future pastors and leaders.

They are ministering to people through chaplaincy, showing up to be present with people in some of the most heartbreaking moments of their lives, sitting in solidarity with the broken, and bringing light and hope to some of the darkest places.

They are ministering in small churches, doing so many unseen tasks to keep their churches alive and well, faithfully serving in profound ways.

They are ministering in large churches, thoughtfully and courageously leading their teams well.

They are ministering through nonstandard expressions of church, reimagining the very shape of what a faith community can be in a rapidly changing world.

They are ministering creatively through art and music, sharing the truth that worship is using all of our selves in beautiful ways.

There is not enough room or time to list all the names and places and ways that God is calling and using women in faithful service to share the good news with the world. This isn't a full snapshot of women in church leadership. Women are serving in every ministry space imaginable, often carving that space for themselves through church planting and creative ministry.

God is still calling women to preach, to teach, to write, to lead. The Holy Spirit is still empowering and equipping women leaders. As Psalm 68:11 tells us, "The Lord announces the word, and the women who proclaim it are a mighty throng." May we listen and follow these women as they lead, and may we be a people who do not hinder the work of God in our midst but make way for the Spirit of God to move mightily.

QUESTIONS FOR DISCUSSION OR REFLECTION

1. Whose story from this chapter stands out the most to you? Why does that one connect with you?

2. How did you feel reading about the drop-off in women clergy in the 1920s, '30s, and '40s in the United States? What does this say about how easily we can open or close the doors for the girls and women in our midst who may be called by God to the ministry? What obstacles might remain in the path of women today who are called by God?

3. How has your own life been impacted by the leadership of women in the church—or by an absence of women in leadership in the church?

4. What women in your life have taught, preached to, or cared for you?

5. Think about your own life. While you might not be called to vocational ministry, God is calling you to faithfully serve him in *some* way. Where might God be calling you, and how does God want to use you?

6. What is one way you can advocate or care for women leaders in the church who feel that there are challenges for them around every corner? How can you be an advocate for a church where women and men work together as an image of the beautiful, diverse kingdom of God on earth?

SUGGESTIONS FOR FURTHER READING

Lynn Cohick and Amy Brown Hughes, *Christian Women in the Patristic World: Their Influence, Authority, and Legacy in the Second through Fifth Centuries* (2017)

Rebecca Laird, *Ordained Women in the Church of the Nazarene: The First Generation* (1993)

Michaele LaVigne, *Living the Way of Jesus: Practicing the Christian Calendar One Week at a Time* (2019)

Susie Stanley, *Holy Boldness: Women Preachers' Autobiographies and the Sanctified Self* (2004)

Carla D. Sunberg, *Uncommon Virtues: Seven Saints Who Shaped Our Faith* (2018)

Carla D. Sunberg, ed., *Faithful to the Call: Women in Ministry* (2022)

Simone Twibell, *Intimacy with God: An Invitation to Prayer* (2023)

Mildred Bangs Wynkoop, *A Theology of Love: The Dynamic of Wesleyanism* (1972; 2015)

BIBLIOGRAPHY

←→

Bergen, Raquel Kennedy and Elizabeth Barnhill. "Marital Rape, New Research and Directions." VAWnet: The National Online Resource Center on Violence against Women (February 2006).

Claassens, Juliana. "Calling the Keeners: The Image of the Wailing Woman as Symbol of Survival in a Traumatized World." *Journal of Feminist Studies in Religion*, n.d.

Clark-Soles, Jaime. *Women in the Bible: Resources for the Use of Scripture in the Church.* Louisville: Westminster John Knox Press, 2020.

Cohick, Lynn H. *The Letter to the Ephesians.* New International Commentary on the New Testament. Grand Rapids: Eerdmans, 2020.

Cohick, Lynn H. and Amy Brown Hughes. *Christian Women in the Patristic World: Their Influence, Authority, and Legacy in the Second through Fifth Centuries.* Grand Rapids: Baker Academic, 2017.

Coleson, Joseph. *Genesis 1–11.* New Beacon Bible Commentary. Kansas City, MO: Beacon Hill Press of Kansas City, 2012.

Derck, Sarah B. C., Joseph Coleson, and Elaine Bernius. *Ruth, Song of Songs, Esther.* New Beacon Bible Commentary. Kansas City, MO: Beacon Hill Press of Kansas City, 2020.

Gupta, Nijay K. *Tell Her Story: How Women Led, Taught, and Ministered in the Early Church.* Downers Grove, IL: InterVarsity Press, 2023.

Hunter, Fannie McDowell. *Women Preachers.* Dallas: Berachah Printing Company, 1905.

Hylen, Susan E. *A Modest Apostle: Thecla and the History of Women in the Early Church.* Oxford: Oxford University Press, 2015.

————. *Women in the New Testament World*. New York: Oxford University Press, 2019.

Laird, Rebecca. *Ordained Women in the Church of the Nazarene: The First Generation*. Kansas City, MO: Nazarene Publishing House, 1993.

Lyons, George, Robert W. Smith, and Kara Lyons-Pardue. *Ephesians, Colossians, Philemon*. New Beacon Bible Commentary. Kansas City, MO: Beacon Hill Press of Kansas City, 2019.

McKnight, Scot. *John*. New Testament Everyday Bible Study. Grand Rapids: HarperChristian Resources, 2022.

Morgan, Timothy C. "The Stained-Glass Ceiling." *Christianity Today* (May 16, 1994).

Peppiatt, Lucy. *Rediscovering Scripture's Vision for Women*. Downers Grove, IL: InterVarsity Press, 2019.

————. *Women and Worship at Corinth*. Eugene, OR: Cascade Books, 2015.

Pokrifka, H. Junia. *Exodus*. New Beacon Bible Commentary. Kansas City, MO: Beacon Hill Press of Kansas City, 2018.

Stanley, Susie C. *Holy Boldness: Women Preachers' Autobiographies*. Knoxville, TN: University of Tennessee Press, 2004.

Taylor, Joan E. and Helen Bond. *Women Remembered*. London: Hodder & Stoughton, 2023.

Taylor, Joan E. and Ilaria L. E. Ramelli, eds. *Patterns of Women's Leadership in Early Christianity*. New York: Oxford University Press, 2021.

www.ingramcontent.com/pod-product-compliance
Lightning Source LLC
LaVergne TN
LVHW051558080426
835510LV00020B/3034